French Philosophy: A Very Short Introduction

VERY SHORT INTRODUCTIONS are for anyone wanting a stimulating and accessible way into a new subject. They are written by experts, and have been translated into more than 45 different languages.

The series began in 1995, and now covers a wide variety of topics in every discipline. The VSI library currently contains over 650 volumes—a Very Short Introduction to everything from Psychology and Philosophy of Science to American History and Relativity—and continues to grow in every subject area.

Very Short Introductions available now:

ABOLITIONISM Richard S. Newman
THE ABRAHAMIC RELIGIONS
    Charles L. Cohen
ACCOUNTING Christopher Nobes
ADAM SMITH Christopher J. Berry
ADOLESCENCE Peter K. Smith
ADVERTISING Winston Fletcher
AERIAL WARFARE
    Frank Ledwidge
AESTHETICS Bence Nanay
AFRICAN AMERICAN RELIGION
    Eddie S. Glaude Jr
AFRICAN HISTORY John Parker
    and Richard Rathbone
AFRICAN POLITICS Ian Taylor
AFRICAN RELIGIONS
    Jacob K. Olupona
AGEING Nancy A. Pachana
AGNOSTICISM Robin Le Poidevin
AGRICULTURE Paul Brassley and
    Richard Soffe
ALBERT CAMUS Oliver Gloag
ALEXANDER THE GREAT
    Hugh Bowden
ALGEBRA Peter M. Higgins
AMERICAN BUSINESS HISTORY
    Walter A. Friedman
AMERICAN CULTURAL HISTORY
    Eric Avila
AMERICAN FOREIGN RELATIONS
    Andrew Preston
AMERICAN HISTORY Paul S. Boyer
AMERICAN IMMIGRATION
    David A. Gerber

AMERICAN LEGAL HISTORY
    G. Edward White
AMERICAN NAVAL HISTORY
    Craig L. Symonds
AMERICAN POLITICAL HISTORY
    Donald Critchlow
AMERICAN POLITICAL PARTIES
    AND ELECTIONS L. Sandy Maisel
AMERICAN POLITICS
    Richard M. Valelly
THE AMERICAN PRESIDENCY
    Charles O. Jones
THE AMERICAN REVOLUTION
    Robert J. Allison
AMERICAN SLAVERY
    Heather Andrea Williams
THE AMERICAN WEST Stephen Aron
AMERICAN WOMEN'S HISTORY
    Susan Ware
ANAESTHESIA Aidan O'Donnell
ANALYTIC PHILOSOPHY
    Michael Beaney
ANARCHISM Colin Ward
ANCIENT ASSYRIA Karen Radner
ANCIENT EGYPT Ian Shaw
ANCIENT EGYPTIAN ART AND
    ARCHITECTURE Christina Riggs
ANCIENT GREECE Paul Cartledge
THE ANCIENT NEAR EAST
    Amanda H. Podany
ANCIENT PHILOSOPHY Julia Annas
ANCIENT WARFARE
    Harry Sidebottom
ANGELS David Albert Jones

Available soon:

For more information visit our website

www.oup.com/vsi/

Stephen Gaukroger and Knox Peden

FRENCH
PHILOSOPHY

A Very Short Introduction

OXFORD
UNIVERSITY PRESS

OXFORD
UNIVERSITY PRESS

Great Clarendon Street, Oxford, OX2 6DP,
United Kingdom

Oxford University Press is a department of the University of Oxford.
It furthers the University's objective of excellence in research, scholarship,
and education by publishing worldwide. Oxford is a registered trade mark of
Oxford University Press in the UK and in certain other countries

© Stephen Gaukroger and Knox Peden 2020

The moral rights of the authors have been asserted

First edition published in 2020

Impression: 2

Published in the United States of America by Oxford University Press
198 Madison Avenue, New York, NY 10016, United States of America

British Library Cataloguing in Publication Data
Data available

Library of Congress Control Number: 2020932754

ISBN 978-0-19-882917-1

Printed in Great Britain by
Ashford Colour Press Ltd, Gosport, Hampshire

Contents

Contents

Chapter 1
Introduction

French culture is unique in that philosophy has played a significant role from the early-modern period onwards, intimately associated with political, religious, and literary debates as well as with epistemological and scientific ones. While Latin was the language of learning there was a universal philosophical literature. However, with the rise of vernacular literatures, a distinctive national form of philosophy arose in France, although major figures in French 17th-century philosophy, Gassendi and Descartes, both published works first in Latin (in Descartes' case quickly followed by French versions).

The first philosophical work written in French was Montaigne's *Essays* (1580). Writing in the vernacular was in itself a radical move, as Latin was not only the language of scholarship, but in Catholic countries it was regarded as the sacred language. The Church saw European nations as being a single family under the headship of the Pope, and Latin as the common language of this family. Montaigne's father had made sure that his son's first language was Latin, and in 17th-century colleges, such as the one Descartes would attend, speaking in French was punished: Latin was the language of the literate. But this does not mean that French was the language of the illiterate. In France at the time of the Revolution, the French language was dominant in only fifteen of the country's eighty-nine departments, sharing the stage with

German, as well as Basque, Breton, Occitan, Provençal, and other patois. One of the great crusades of the early Revolution was, in fact, to make French the language of France. In the 18th century, French came to replace Latin as the language of scholarship, and this meant that some philosophers who were not French wrote in the language: Leibniz, who was German, wrote one of his major works in French, for example. So 'French philosophy' is not quite so straightforward before the 19th century, but the work of Francophone philosophers, even if they occasionally wrote in Latin, is nevertheless distinctive, and this distinctiveness is what we have set out to trace.

'Philosophy' in the early-modern period was something that included natural philosophy ('science') and theology as well as metaphysics and ethics. From the middle of the 18th century it became closely affiliated with radical political positions, in thinkers such as Voltaire and Diderot, and played an important role in the shaping of the French Revolution. The Revolution in turn provided a point of reference for 19th-century thinkers such as Comte, who offered an account of science and politics ('sociology') on a new 'positivist' basis.

Although philosophy became professionalized in France later in the 19th century, it was never on the theologically orientated German model, and by contrast with Anglophone philosophy, it remained of significance in French cultural life outside academia. The *philosophe* of the Enlightenment morphed into the figure of the intellectual who emerged in the Belle Époque and remains continuous with that of the 'public intellectual' we recognize today.

The early 20th century saw the refashioning of 19th-century tendencies. Spiritualism laid the ground for the vitalism promoted by Henri Bergson. And Comtean rationalism led to the emergence of a science-friendly neo-Kantianism in the highest echelons of French academic philosophy. Cross-cutting these intellectual commitments were positions on the status of the French Republic and its relationship to Catholic modes of thought. The First World War was a watershed in that it shattered a younger generation's confidence in the political and philosophical wisdom of its elders, on the right and the left. In its wake, a series of philosophers from Germany and further east introduced phenomenology and other existentialist traditions into French philosophy. These new ideas were taken up with much enthusiasm.

The story of 20th-century French philosophy is one of reckoning, on the one hand with the impact of external developments—above all German phenomenology—but also with an inheritance profoundly devoted to the history of philosophy as a humanistic discipline and a seemingly perennial conflict between secular and religious tendencies in the tradition. Persistent throughout this history has been philosophy's culturally privileged relationship to politics in France and particularly radical left-wing politics. The impact of 'French Theory' on the wider world has shaped our understanding of the internal developments of recent French thought by focusing attention on the relationship between structuralism and post-structuralism. But a guiding thread of this recent history has been the dilemma sustained by a markedly national conception of philosophy and philosophical culture that nevertheless arrogates to itself a right and capacity to speak to matters of universal concern.

Much of the grandeur of French philosophy stems from this sense of vocation that stretches back to ancient Greece. But this virtue can also be a vice in that it can sometimes place a premium on innovation (or the appearance of it) at the expense of other values. Nevertheless, the focus on themes that have been in conflict throughout the history of Western modernity makes French philosophy a privileged place from which to think about that history. Much as French politics has long served as, at once, the mirror and the alternative to the vicissitudes of Anglophone liberalism, French philosophy tends to elicit strong reactions on the part of Anglophone readers. In this book, we approach French philosophy through its history, but we also aim to provide summaries of important thinkers and texts. French philosophy is often as challenging as it is beguiling. Our hope is that this book will show that engagement with it is also ultimately rewarding, and will encourage readers to explore it more fully for themselves.

Chapter 2
The origins of French philosophy

Montaigne

Although, in university and college philosophy courses, French philosophy is generally taken to start with Descartes, it actually begins fifty years earlier with the *Essays* (1580) of Montaigne (1533–92). Moreover, while the best-known works of Descartes (1595–1650) such as the *Meditations* and the *Principles of Philosophy* first appeared in Latin, the *Essays* were written in French. Francophone philosophy effectively began with Montaigne. Yet Montaigne's contribution inhabits a grey area. On the one hand, it is very much in the genre of Renaissance humanist writing, combining moral, psychological, and literary concerns, largely shaped by Stoic philosophy, and containing anecdotes and autobiographical fragments as well as considered discussion of philosophical issues. On the other hand, it initiates a discussion of the nature of knowledge and belief that was to shape the kind of modern philosophy that we associate with Descartes and his successors.

How did this transition come about? Montaigne's *Essays* are an exercise in self-exploration, and began in a humanist mode whose aim was the discovery of a universal human nature. But what he ended up doing was something completely different. He discovered himself, his thoughts, feelings, emotions: something cut off not just from the empirical world but from other subjects. It is not that *subjectivity* conceived as a universal human nature is cut off from empirical nature, but rather that the *self* is cut off from empirical nature and indeed from other selves. Descartes will deploy this view of the self—a self that has an identity in its own right, independent of the relation in which it stands either to the empirical world or to other selves—in an epistemological context, so that the locus of knowledge of the empirical world is now something removed from the empirical world. The transition between what Montaigne is doing and what Descartes is doing is not continuous however, and there are two sharp differences between Montaigne and fully-fledged modern philosophy of the kind that we find in Descartes.

The first concerns scepticism. Montaigne is often taken to have been the first to formulate scepticism in modern philosophy, but what he actually offered was something of a mixture of scepticism and relativism. The sceptic argues that there is a way that the world is—it contains definite things organized in a definite way, for example—but we cannot know how it is. The relativist, by contrast, argues that there is no way that the world is: there are different views of the world which just depend on the interests and values of the person who has those theories, and none is better than any other. For example, in the essay usually identified as Montaigne's statement of scepticism, the 'Apology for Raymond Sebond', the examples that he gives—what is true on one side of the mountain is false on the other; we hide away while engaging in sexual intercourse whereas the Indians have sex in public— suggest relativism rather than scepticism. Montaigne's disciple, Pierre Charron (1541–1603), in his very popular *On Wisdom* (1601), reinforces this reading, telling us that human reason is a 'wandering, changeable, distorting, variable implement'; that there is no reason which does not have its opposite; and that 'what is an abomination in one place is piety in another'. But if Montaigne does not clearly distinguish scepticism from relativism,

6

Descartes definitely does, and scepticism is crucial for his epistemological programme.

The second feature of Montaigne's philosophy is that questions that have subsequently been regarded as epistemological were treated in a mixture of psychological and epistemological terms, in very much a humanist vein. This genre gives moral questions, and above all that of how to live one's life, a central place. Descartes is certainly concerned with these questions, particularly later in his life, but his principal concern is with natural philosophy and its epistemological defence, and moral questions tend to fit awkwardly into how he does philosophy, running the risk of becoming added extras.

Gassendi

Nevertheless, the line between Montaigne's humanist approach and Descartes' focus on natural philosophy is not absolute. In many respects Descartes' near contemporary Pierre Gassendi (1592–1655) pursued a middle ground between the two. Although Gassendi's natural philosophy takes the form of a systematic matter theory—with Cartesianism, it was one of the two great mechanist systems of the second half of the 17th century—he came to natural philosophy via a very different route from Descartes, through humanist studies, and his approach could not be further from that of Descartes. One of his prime concerns is to build up detailed historical evidence for his natural-philosophical position, something wholly alien to Descartes' approach. His aim was to establish that atomism had been the pre-eminent natural-philosophical tradition in antiquity, and to show in detail how this had been obscured by a combination of slander and mistaken criticisms, mainly at the hands of Aristotle. In this way it becomes clear, he argues, that atomism, not Aristotelianism, is the most viable natural-philosophical system, and as a consequence it is atomism that is the appropriate partner for Christianity.

Gassendi's Christianized Epicureanism was in the genre of Christianized Aristotelianism and Christianized neo-Platonism, and a good deal of the effort went into compromises and revisions that enabled systems that were in many respects disparate and contradictory to be reconciled. To some extent, this was a success and Gassendism vied successfully with Cartesianism as the dominant natural philosophy until the end of the 17th century.

Descartes

Descartes stands at the origins of modern philosophy in the way that Plato stood at the origins of ancient philosophy. Both of them fashioned the subject, set out the basic problems, and offered solutions which others subsequently argued over. Disputes over the interpretation of Descartes helped shape French thought throughout the 18th and 19th centuries. But his concerns differed somewhat from the investments made in his work by philosophers in later centuries. In particular, like his contemporaries, his principal concerns lay in natural philosophy—in mathematics, the physical sciences, and the life sciences—although it was his foray into epistemology that secured his reputation in later centuries.

Descartes' early interests were in mathematics. Around 1619, he began to reflect on an instrument called the proportional compass: a compass with four limbs, marked out in units, joined in such a way that opening the compass allows one to read off proportional relationships. What was interesting about the compass was that it enabled one to deal with an arithmetical problem, namely the calculation of compound interest, and a geometrical one, the trisection of an angle. Arithmetic and geometry had always been treated as distinct autonomous disciplines, dealing with discontinuous and continuous magnitudes respectively. But here was a device that spanned both, and Descartes realized that the theory of proportions was a mathematical discipline that subsumed both arithmetic and geometry. Developing the theory of proportions, Descartes moves to what he called 'universal mathematics'—basically a form of algebra, an even more powerful super-discipline that would encompass all particular quantitative disciplines, including such areas as geometrical optics and acoustics. From this he postulated the most general such discipline, the 'universal method', supposedly offering a method of discovery in any area. At the same time, Descartes was working on optics, trying to discover what shape of lens would reduce distortion, and in the course of this work he discovered the sine law of refraction: the law that describes the bending of a light ray as it moves from one medium to another. When not working in optics, he pursued physiology, and is generally credited with the discovery of reflex action.

By the late 1620s, Descartes began to take a serious interest in the nature of matter and motion, developing an ingenious defence of the heliocentric theory: the theory that the earth rotates around the sun. He developed an elaborate physical and cosmological account, followed by an equally ambitious account of physiology which construed all physiological process in mechanical terms, that is, in terms of matter in motion. But at the end of 1633 he learned of the Church's condemnation of Galileo, and, unable to publish, he put his work to one side. The core of the Church's argument had been that natural philosophy, the standing of which was hypothetical, could not be used to establish heliocentrism in the face of scriptural authority. In other words, the basic problem was the hypothetical standing of natural philosophy. Descartes' response was to ask how a natural philosophy might shed its hypothetical status, and this prompted him to ask whether there was any type of knowledge that could command absolute certainty.

He found the answer in devising a form of scepticism that was quite new. Compared to earlier forms of scepticism it had two distinctive features: it concerned knowledge claims; and it was hyperbolic, that is, it was directed towards things about which one felt certain. On the first question, ancient scepticism had not been directed at knowledge claims, but at things that one believed. The ancient sceptics, the Pyrrhonists, challenged beliefs. They set out to show that for any given belief, there were equally compelling reasons to hold its opposite. Consequently, there was no reason to hold one belief rather than another. Descartes was not concerned with beliefs. For him we are entitled to our beliefs, so long as we do not claim the title of knowledge for them. It is our claims to know things that he is interested in, and his argument is that what we can doubt is far more widespread than had been thought. Hyperbolic doubt questions things of which one is certain: for example, that we have bodies or that there is an external physical world. In order to understand on what grounds Descartes could envisage such doubt, we need to turn to his understanding of the nature of God's powers. Christians believed that God was omnipotent, although medieval theologians occasionally struggled with logical problems to do with omnipotence—such as whether God could create a stone that was too heavy even for him to lift. Some medieval theologians believed that God's omnipotence extended to logical and mathematical truths, that he could change basic truths of arithmetic, making 2 plus 2 equal 5, for example. Descartes' view was that although we might not even be able to comprehend what it would it be like for 2 plus 2 to equal 5, what we can comprehend cannot limit the powers of an omniscient and omnipotent God. In the *Meditations* (1641), Descartes transfers hyperbolic doubt from God into what he calls 'an evil demon', a hypothetical entity that is able to mislead us about our most fundamental knowledge claims, including those about which we can be absolutely certain. But, famously, there is one claim that cannot be damaged by such doubt, knowledge of my own existence, for from the very fact of doubting it follows that there must be someone who is doing the doubting.

In the *Meditations*, the theory of knowledge, epistemology, takes centre stage in philosophy for the first time, and it does so in an especially dramatic form, offering a mental purging of a kind previously only encountered in religious literature. It puts the knowing subject on the spot, demanding that any knowledge claim, even the seemingly most trivial or obvious, be justified, and this demand for justification is presented as if one's life depended on it: for Descartes wants us to show us that our cognitive life does indeed depend on it. The *Meditations* aim to make one responsible for one's cognitive life in a way that the devotional texts of the Reformation and Counter-Reformation—where a range of exacting moral standards, accompanied by demands for self-vigilance which had been the preserve of monastic culture throughout the Middle Ages, were transferred wholesale to the general populace—made one responsible for the minute details of one's everyday life. Philosophy becomes personal with Descartes. It is no longer the preserve of, or exclusively of concern to, the cleric. Indeed, Descartes' view is that the person best fitted to be a philosopher is someone whose mind has not been corrupted by scholastic learning. The nature of philosophy is transformed, although it does in some ways return to the notion of the philosopher as portrayed by Socrates in Plato's early dialogues, someone who has had no special training but takes nothing on trust, subjecting everything to intense examination and questioning.

This indubitable knowledge that Descartes discovers now acts as a model, and as a basis for discovering how one builds up knowledge claims such that they remain free of doubt. The aim is not to re-establish the claims that have been overturned by hyperbolic doubt, however, but rather to establish a criterion by which we can recognize genuine knowledge, namely that of 'clarity and distinctness'. Only if I can conceive of something clearly and distinctly am I entitled to call it knowledge; and when it comes to the physical world, my only route to clear and distinct conceptions is via mathematics. Reconstructing the world of mathematical grounds is the work of Descartes' *Principles of Philosophy* (1644), which starts by recapitulating the argument of the *Meditations*— which had always only been a preparation for the *Principles*—and then using this to establish his theory of matter and motion; then moving to show how one can demonstrate that the earth and the planets must rotate around the sun; and how it could not be otherwise.

But much as Descartes is concerned to move on from doubting to constructing a scientific image of the natural world, it informs the conclusions he comes to on a host of other fundamental questions. In the first instance, what the doubt pushes us into is subjectivity, and indeed epistemological doubt centres on the perspective of the subject. Ancient scepticism, Pyrrhonism, had made constant reference to subjective states, and indeed it made what one believes relative to a whole range of subjective states—anger, love, familiarity, habits, religious views, and so on—which Descartes never even mentions. Yet he manages to make the whole question of legitimation turn around the subject. Although he is concerned with such questions as that of what in perception is due to the perceiver and what is due to the world, this in itself would not generate a concern with subjectivity. Pyrrhonism did not end up distancing us from the world, for example; on the contrary, it shows that we are so integrated with the world that its very particular features shape our experience of it, making it impossible to transcend this particularity by trying to find optimal conditions for cognition.

Cartesian doubt pushes us in the other direction, and Descartes achieves this by developing and transforming Montaigne's conception of subjectivity. At the same time, he manages to transform, in a far more decisive way than any of his predecessors or contemporaries, the aim of metaphysics by changing the question of how the world is into that of how the world is *independently of us*. This makes an investigation of 'us' mandatory. By asking how the world is independently of us, rather than just how the world is, an epistemological ingredient is built into metaphysics that was not there previously. What Descartes does is to approach the question of how the world is independently of us by exploring the nature of the subject's experience and asking what features of that experience entitle us to make claims to knowledge. It will be helpful to distinguish four aspects of Descartes' conception.

First, Descartes assumes that, even in doubting, I cannot doubt that there is something that is doing the doubting, and he proceeds to ask for the nature of this doubting subject. The key assumption here is that there is what we might refer to as a unified locus of subjectivity, a self, which is the origin or bearer of the particular doubt. Such a conception of subjectivity had been questioned by the Andalusian philosopher Averroes (1126–98), and these debates were still alive in the 17th century. Averroes had argued that there can only be one intellect in the universe, which precludes the intellect being identified with an individual self, as Descartes maintains. As the Renaissance philosopher Zabarella (1533–89) describes it, the intellect

> is not multiplied in accordance with the number of men but is only one in number in the whole human species.... When any man dies, this Intellect does not perish but remains the same in number in those that are left.

The motivation behind this account of the mind derived from the Aristotelian doctrine that pure form cannot be individuated, and it was concluded from this that disembodied minds cannot be individuated and cannot be more than one in number. The theological problem with this is that, while it allows immortality, it does not allow personal immortality.

This brings us to the second issue, the question of Descartes' identification of the self with something intellectual, namely the mind. Descartes does two things here: he argues that the mind must be spiritual, and he assumes that having shown this he has also shown that the mind is identical with the self. Both of these are questionable. The way in which he establishes the first is a disaster. His argument is that I can doubt whether my body exists without doubting whether I exist, so the existence of my body cannot be the same as the existence of me. In the fourth set of objections to the *Meditations*, Arnauld points out that this reasoning is quite invalid. For consider a parallel case. I may well be able to doubt that a right-angled triangle has the property of having a hypotenuse whose square is equal to the sum of the squares of the other sides; but it does not follow from my being able to doubt that a right-angled triangle has this property that it does not really have it. In a somewhat tortuous reply, Descartes effectively concedes the point, maintaining that the real demonstration of the distinctness of mind and body comes only in Meditation 6, although the 'demonstration' given there simply states that I have a clear and distinct idea of mind, as something thinking and unextended, and I have a clear and distinct idea of body, as something non-thinking and extended, so the two cannot be the same. There is also a deeper question at stake: to identify the mind with 'thought' is not automatically to identify it with the self. The key doctrines condemned by the Church had been Averroism and Alexandrism. Both of these had offered a doctrine on the question of the nature of the mind and had maintained that while the corporeal faculties were active the individual mind acted by means of those faculties. Alexandrians had argued that these corporeal faculties must be constitutive of the mind, because forms must always be instantiated in matter. Consequently, once the corporeal faculties ceased to be active, at death, the form of the body, its soul, also ceased to exist. One way around this conclusion, for a Christian Aristotelian, was to stress the doctrine of the resurrection of the body at the Last Judgement. One's mind/form was then reunited with one's (revamped) body. There were metaphysical problems with this account, however, which centred on what happened between death and the Last Judgement: most notably, what happened to the form (which cannot exist uninstantiated) in the meantime, and whether the entity who reappeared at the Last Judgement could be said to be the same person as the one who had died earlier. Tying the mind/soul to a body was clearly fraught with problems. On the other hand, to dissociate the mind from the body, as the Averroists did, was equally problematic, for it led to an inability to individuate minds, and to their identification with one another and perhaps even ultimately with God. Alexandrism and Averroism are the competing dangers through which Descartes must steer a passage in setting out his doctrine of the nature of the mind. In this, he faces insuperable difficulties.

Third, there is the question of what is included in the 'thinking' that the thinking subject, the *res cogitans*, engages in. It is clear from his earlier *Treatise on Man*, that Descartes must allow some kind of thinking to animals in as much as they are capable of perceptual discrimination, but the 'thinking' that is at issue here in the *Meditations* is something in which the mind proper engages, and not something that animals are capable of. One possible distinguishing feature is that human sense perception involves an awareness of one's perceptual states as perceptual states, whereas animal sense perception does not. There can be no doubt that Descartes believes that this is the case. The question is whether this in itself is all there is to it. What is so special about a simple awareness of one's own mental states? There is a widespread view that Descartes thought that awareness of one's own mental states was in fact constitutive of the uniqueness of human cognition. But is consciousness of one's mental states, in Descartes' view, constitutive of human mental life or is such consciousness merely what is required if human mental life is to possess the features traditionally ascribed to it, namely will and judgement? What makes human beings capable of judgement and volition is the fact that they can reflect on their own mental states, whereas animals cannot. Such traditional mental functions require awareness of one's own mental states, and this awareness is distinctive of human cognition and absent from animals, but it is not constitutive of them. The most sensible reading of Descartes' claim is correspondingly that awareness of one's own mental states is the key to the difference between creatures with a mind and animals, and that without such awareness the characteristic features of human mental life would not be possible.

Fourth, there is the question of the nature of the relation between the mind and the body. In Meditation 6, Descartes criticizes a form of Platonic dualism, pointing out that:

> Nature teaches me through the sensations of hunger and thirst etc. that I am not merely present in my body as a sailor is present in a ship, but that I am very closely joined, and as it were intermingled, with it, so that I and the body form a unity.

Sensory awareness is neither straightforwardly bodily nor straightforwardly intellectual. Later, Descartes will maintain that there are three 'primitive' categories: extension, thought, and the 'substantial union of mind and body', showing just how seriously he takes the question.

The relation between the mind and the body is a question that impinges on two rather different projects for Descartes. The first is the establishment of the immortality of the soul. Here Descartes is unqualifiedly dualist. The second is the understanding of cognition and the passions of the soul: here Descartes' account works exclusively in terms of an embodied mind, and we get no idea what a disembodied mind would be like. Now you can be a kind of dualist and argue that, although mind and body are separate substances, mind must always be instantiated in matter. This is not Descartes' view, but when it comes to his discussion of cognition and the passions, one could be forgiven for thinking it was. The questions are complicated by Descartes' introduction, in his correspondence with Princess Elizabeth of Bohemia (1618–80), of the idea of the substantial union of mind and body, that is, the doctrine that as well as mind and body, we should consider the union of the two as a kind of third entity. In a letter to Elizabeth, he refers to 'three kinds of primitive notions', namely the mind, the body, and the union of the two. To put the issue in more modern terms, we should think in terms of a tripartite distinction between: disembodied mind, body, and embodied mind.

There were two directions in which Descartes could have gone in response to the problems. The first is to sever the connection between mind and body, advocating a form of occasionalism, the doctrine that mind and body act in tandem rather than acting causally upon one another. The second is to make the connection between operations of mind and body closer than one might otherwise have expected in a dualist account, through the doctrine of the substantial union.

When faced with the question of how the mind and the body interact, Descartes took the option of the substantial union of mind and body rather than the occasionalist route. The substantial union doctrine minimizes the ontological gap between mind and body, trying to de-problematize their interaction in this way. The occasionalist solution takes the opposite path. It accepts that there is an unbridgeable gap between mind and body, and shows how events at one level are accompanied by, but not causally effected by, events at another. It does this because the occasionalist denies any causation at the natural level, whether of a mind/body kind or a body/body kind. As regards the relation between mind and body, it asks us to imagine two levels of events—one physical one mental—running in tandem, but not interacting with one another. How can this happen, you might ask? On the occasionalist account, there is no causal process between one physical object and another, there are no causal processes between mind and body, and there are no causal processes between minds. Only God can cause anything. Think about how we might describe events in these terms. A knife enters your leg and you feel pain. On the occasionalist view, God causes the knife to enter your leg, and he causes the physical wound; and he also causes the pain. It's not the wound that causes the pain, but God causing a particular mental state whenever he causes a particular bodily state.

17

You might think that this is a particularly uneconomical way for God to proceed. But you must remember that, if one accepts the personal immortality of a purely spiritual soul, as the occasionalists generally did, then in considering our interaction with other things, our time on earth attached to a body is infinitesimally small, and our time in heaven (or elsewhere) infinitely long. It's also worth remembering that many philosophers who were not occasionalists, and indeed who did not invoke God in their accounts, shared with occasionalists concerns about physical causation and about psychophysical causation. In the first case they argued that bodies do not have any power by which to affect other bodies, and that there are no real causes in nature: bodies simply obey general laws, they do not really act on one another. Second, some philosophers, despairing of any solution to how minds and brains can interact, have simply dispensed with minds, arguing that they can be reduced to brains.

Malebranche

The great defender of occasionalism was Malebranche. His *Search for Truth*, which first appeared in 1674, dominated philosophical thought in the final quarter of the 17th century, being eclipsed only at the end of that century by Locke's *Essay*. Malebranche saw himself as a Cartesian, as developing a core strand of thought in Descartes in a more logical and more fully-worked out way. But he was also committed to the writings of St Augustine. Augustinianism experienced something of a revival in France in the middle of the 17th century. Blaise Pascal (1623–62) had stressed the fallen nature of human beings, and the limits that this placed on their ability to understand. The limits were severe and those who had ignored them were irresponsible, on Pascal's view. His scepticism towards reason and its demonstrative capacities led Pascal to conceive of faith as a kind of decision, the result of a 'wager' on the essential order of the universe that later thinkers would regard as proto-existentialist. As for philosophy, one possible remedy lay in the Augustinian doctrine of divine illumination, which in Pascal's thought manifested as an emphasis on grace. On this account, just as natural objects need to be illuminated if we are to be able to see them, so too must truths be illuminated by a kind of spiritual light if we are to be able to grasp them. The source of corporeal illumination is the sun; but the source of spiritual illumination is God.

The combination of Cartesianism and Augustinianism leads to somewhat novel doctrines in Malebranche. Descartes had three different kinds of substance: infinite substance (God), finite spiritual substance (mind), and finite extended substance (matter), but he provides no discussion of the systematic relations between the three. Malebranche does, as for him this is where the key to the whole thing lies, and Malebranche is nothing if not systematic. He has effectively two substances, God and matter, with mind somewhere in the middle. Mind is a kind of intermediary between God and matter, which are wholly distinct from one another. It either shares in God, insofar as it is pure intellect, or shares in matter, insofar as it is attached to a body. Finally, it depends for its existence on God but not on its union with matter: it can be separated from body, but it would cease to exist without God.

In the Preface to the *Search after Truth*, Malebranche puts it in these terms:

> The mind of man is by nature situated, as it were, between its creator and corporeal creatures, for, according to St Augustine, there is nothing but God above it and nothing but bodies below it. But as the mind's position above all material things does not prevent it from being joined to them, and even depending in a way on a part of matter, so the infinite distance between the sovereign being and the mind of man does not prevent it from being immediately joined to it in a very intimate way. The latter union raises the mind above all things. Through it the mind receives its life, its light, and its entire felicity, and at many points in his works

St. Augustine speaks of this union as the one most natural and essential to the mind. The mind's union with the body, on the other hand, infinitely debases man and is today the main cause of all his errors and miseries.

The bulk of the *Search after Truth*—that is, five of the six books— is devoted to an account of how these errors due to the mind's union with the body arise. We can focus on one of these errors, which concerns sensation.

On Malebranche's account, the senses are *not* designed to reveal to us the nature of the external world. That is not their function. Their function is simply to notify us—that is, our minds—of our bodily needs in a quick and economical way. Before the Fall, Adam had grasped this and he never relied on his senses to judge the nature of bodies. But since the Fall we have become very dependent on our bodies. This, Malebranche considers, is disastrous, because our senses are intrinsically untrustworthy.

He distinguishes between our judgement of primary qualities and our judgement of secondary qualities, and denies that the senses are trustworthy guides to the discovery of such primary qualities of objects as size, shape, motion, and location. But we are not *completely* deceived about the characteristics of bodies, for we are right in believing that bodies have some size, shape, location, speed, and direction of movement, even if we are wrong in supposing them to have the ones they appear to our senses to have. The deception worked on our senses is much more complete in the case of the secondary qualities such as colour, warmth, sound, odour, texture, etc. These, Malebranche tells us, 'in fact are not and never were outside us'.

Our mistakes in this respect arise because we confuse four things: (1) the *action* of an object on our sense organ (e.g. the pressing of the minute parts of a body against our skin); (2) the effect this motion has in our body (e.g. the transmission of impulses from our nerve endings to our brain); (3) the modification of our *mind* that accompanies the event that occurs in our brain (e.g. the feeling of warmth); (4) a belief that arises naturally and involuntarily in us about this sensation (e.g. the belief that the warmth we feel is actually in the object touched and in the hand that touches it).

In general, we confuse sensations and the qualities of objects that accompany them. We have a sensation because the minute parts of bodies—such as light corpuscles; or the rapidly vibrating parts of touched objects—come into contact with our body, and because we don't see these minute parts we suppose the sensations— colour in the first case, warmth in the second—to belong to the object sensed. Now it is significant that we don't make this mistake when the cause of the sensation is visible: when we can actually see the blade of a knife that wounds our hand, for example, we don't suppose that the sensation that accompanies it, namely pain, is a quality of the object. So why should we assume that, in the case where it is invisible like the rapid motion of corpuscles, the warmth that we feel is a quality of the object? Malebranche's conclusion is that how far the cause of a sensation is visible can determine whether or not we will take the sensation itself to be a quality of a body.

What exactly is it that deceives us here? Malebranche points out that it is not so much the *senses* as the *natural judgements* that always accompany sensation. He insists that our sensations are always accompanied by certain involuntary judgements, and the purpose of these is the same as that of sensation: they enable the mind to move swiftly to attend to the body's needs. Our involuntary belief that painful and burning sensations belong to some part of our own body, for example, is, while strictly false, nonetheless very useful. Colours, likewise, enable us to pick out distant bodies—such as predators—much more easily than uncoloured bodies would. We go wrong only when we take these involuntary judgements to inform us of the true nature or properties of bodies. Does this mean that God, who gives us our sense organs and the natural judgements accompanying their exercise, is to blame here? No, says Malebranche. If by a voluntary judgement of our own making we endorse the natural judgements aroused in us, then it is us, not God, who is responsible for the deception.

It was Malebranche, rather than Descartes, who convinced generations of philosophers, particularly Berkeley and Hume, both of whom were deeply indebted to Malebranche, that sceptical arguments formed the core of epistemology, and it was from Malebranche, not from Descartes, that 18th-century readers learned their Cartesianism.

Chapter 3
Radical philosophy: the 18th century

With Malebranche, systematic metaphysics had come to a peak in France, and in the early decades of the 18th century it faced a strong and determined reaction, one which quickly overturned the idea that the best way to pursue philosophy was via systematization. The reaction came as the work of the English philosopher John Locke (1632-1704) was taken up in France, and French philosophy in the 18th century remained deeply influenced by Locke. Among the most important issues that were raised were: the nature of language; whether there were innate ideas; whether consideration of the nature of the mind could be confined to the study of healthy minds; what the relation was between reason and sensibility; and whether European philosophy and religion had the universality that they had been assumed to have. But whatever aspects of Lockean thought French philosophers picked up, they shared a core thesis: the belief that it was sensation, not reason, that underpinned our knowledge of the world, and the corresponding rejection of innate ideas. We can call this approach 'sensationalism'.

Rationalism and empiricism

One of the formative texts of the 18th century was the massive multi-volume *Encyclopedia* edited by Denis Diderot (1713–84) and Jean d'Alembert (1717–83), published from the mid-century onwards. The *Encyclopedia* was the epitome of French Enlightenment thought.

In his general proposal for the reform of knowledge in the 'Preliminary Discourse' to the *Encyclopedia*, d'Alembert defends 'reason'—by contrast with religious teaching, for example—as the sole ultimate criterion of judgement, and associates reason with science. On his Lockean sensationalist programme, it is sensation alone that puts us in touch with the world and allows us to preserve our bodies and to provide them with their needs. The ideas generated from sensation can then be combined and connected, and his ultimate model for these connections is derived from the sciences. Once reason and our knowledge of the world have been associated with science, the main task for d'Alembert is the reconstruction of the history of philosophy and science, showing 'the steps by which we arrived at our present state'. What we need, he argues, is 'a historical explanation of the order in which the various parts of our knowledge succeed one another', and this takes the form of a genealogy of reason showing how, in its historical forms, it converges on the project embodied in the *Encyclopedia*, which thereby represents the culmination of human cognitive endeavour and constitutes the starting point for further enquiry.

The journey to science and rationality is, on d'Alembert's account, a tortuous and circuitous one, and not a linear narrative: the antithesis of rationality was not to be found in antiquity, for example, but in the shift from reason to dogma in the Middle Ages. The development of science (natural philosophy) on d'Alembert's account was a slow process, obstructed by scholasticism. In the arts, poets and others had been allowed to celebrate pagan deities 'as a matter of innocent amusement', something that proved fertile ground for the imagination, and which was hardly a threat to Christianity, since no one was going to be led by this to revive the worship of Jupiter and Pluto. But things were different in science. Here, 'it was either understood, or claimed, that blind reason might wound Christianity'. It was in this climate that religion, whose proper domain was restricted to faith and morals, began to take upon itself the teaching of natural philosophy, and the policing of these areas by the Spanish and Roman Inquisitions. But 'whilst ignorant or malevolent enemies thus made open war on science' it continued to be pursued in secret by some 'extraordinary men'. What d'Alembert sets out is a vindication of the Enlightenment project of the *Encyclopedia*. Primarily at issue was the task of establishing a historical sequence in which one can follow a progression that starts with the origins of knowledge and traces a process of growth—while uncovering and analysing various false starts—which can be shown to culminate in the present.

While the 'Preliminary Discourse' is very much in the Lockean tradition in taking sensation as the basis of knowledge, its characterization of philosophy is distinctive and somewhat idiosyncratic. In the first place, it is staunchly anti-system, and offers an explicit defence of eclecticism. In the entry of that title, we are told that:

> The eclectic is a philosopher who, riding roughshod over prejudice, tradition, antiquity, universal consent, authority, in a word everything that subjugates the mass of minds, dares to think for himself, goes back to the clearest and most general principles, examines them, allowing only that which can be demonstrated from his experience and his reason; and having analysed all philosophical systems without any deference of partiality, he constructs a personal and domestic one that belongs to him.

Yet at the same time, it is with the 'Preliminary Discourse' that we first encounter a precursor of the very uneclectic distinction between 'rationalism' and 'empiricism'. A sensationalist philosophy is set out to counter that of Descartes, construing these for the first time as competing systems, and advocating 'empiricism'. On the one hand, this can be seen as an offshoot of the denial of innate ideas, which was an all-or-nothing matter, so if one were arguing against a system that rested on innate ideas, there was some logic in supporting a system that denied their existence. But it hardly coheres with the defence of eclecticism, and is directly contrary to the Lockean origins of sensationalism, where the rejection of a systematic epistemology is paramount. Moreover, when one follows up what empiricism amounts to, for Diderot for example, it is not so much the epistemological doctrine that we normally associate with that name, but is primarily a defence of materialism.

Language and thought

Locke had reflected on the nature of language more seriously than Descartes or Malebranche, but it was in France that one of the most interesting developments of a Lockean-inspired theory of language came. In his 1746 *Essay on the Origin of Human Knowledge*, whose subtitle describes it as being a supplement to Locke's *Essay*, Etienne Bonnet de Condillac (1715–80) set out by far the most sophisticated theory of language to that time, one that was to shape later 18th-century accounts.

Unlike earlier writers, Condillac did not treat linguistic signs as merely a convenient medium in which to express our thoughts. He had no doubt that humans, like animals, can have thoughts without language, but that what makes us distinctively human is language, because it is linguistic signs that provide us with the means to work on our perception of the world in a conscious fashion. The mind would not be what it is without language, and the increasing sophistication of the mind mirrors the increasing sophistication of language. There are two key issues in Condillac's account: the way in which language provides us with a window onto the activities of the mind; and the importance of the origins of language to the study of its significance.

On the first question, it was a central thesis of Condillac's account that there is a fundamental difference between gestures and the primitive signs designating action, on the one hand, and a fully-fledged language on the other. The faculty of reflection was gradually developed as human beings began to free themselves from their environment, to dissociate natural and gestural language from its associative contexts, and to employ arbitrary signs. Natural and gestural signs are immediate and have no internal differentiation, whereas the distinctive feature of fully-fledged language is its linearity: language requires the breaking down of thoughts and ordering them in a linear fashion. One can analyse one's thoughts, and those of others, because one can present them in a structured linear fashion: linearity is a precondition of the reflection that is distinctive of human thought. In short, language does not simply capture thought, but orders it in a distinctive way that enables one to think reflectively. This in turn provides language users with the means to control mental operations such as memory, imagination, and attention.

On the second question, that of the importance of the origins of language to the study of language, the issues were directly concerned with the question of what it takes for something to be a language. Jean-Jacques Rousseau (1712–78), for example, reflecting on Condillac's account, takes up the issue of how the move from primitive sounds to articulate ones could have been possible. He transforms it into a problem that will shape the subsequent discussion of language in the 18th century, that of accounting for the transition from inarticulate cries to articulate language. Rousseau sets out the problem in these terms in *The Inequality of Men*:

> A mother saying to her child the words he was to use in asking her for something, shows how already existing languages are taught, but this cannot be the explanation of how they came into existence. But assume this first difficulty to be resolved. Suppose ourselves, for the moment, to be on this side of the vast gulf that separates a pure

state of nature and that in which languages are necessary, and, admitting this necessity, then ask how they could have begun to be established. Here we have a new and far worse problem, for if men need speech in order to learn to think, they must have been in far greater need of knowing how to think if they were to discover the art of speaking. And although we might conceive how vocal sounds had been taken as the conventional means of interpretation of our ideas, it would still remain for us to discover what could have been the means of interpretation of this convention in the case of those ideas that, answering to no sensible objects, could be indicated by neither gesture nor voice. Given this, we are barely able to offer any supportable conjectures concerning this art by which we communicate our thoughts and establish a connection between our minds.

It is with Condillac and Rousseau that one of the most extensively debated questions of the mid-18th to mid-19th centuries, that of the origins of language, begins.

Sensation and sensibility

The question of the origins of language was mirrored in an even more fundamental question of origins, that of how we can build up knowledge of the world if we have no innate ideas, but must begin with a blank mind (*tabula rasa*). The question preoccupied French thinkers throughout the 18th century, and raised questions not just of knowledge but of sensibility, and ultimately moral and social questions.

Questions of the connection between sensibility and sensation were introduced into French thought in the 1740s in the work of Condillac and the Comte de Buffon (1707–88). Both independently used the image of a human statue which is progressively given sensory faculties, in order to explore just what is needed to produce a conscious self-aware human being. Moreover, both use the thought experiment in the same way, and reach much the same conclusions. The image of the statue should be considered in the context of French Lockeanism, for it provided a means of exploring how one might replace an innate ideas tradition, in which the qualitative difference between mere sensation and perceptual experience comes with innate ideas. Buffon, Condillac, and Diderot all rejected innate ideas, yet each wanted to register the qualitative difference between merely sensing and having an experience of an external world. Sensibility takes on a key role here, since for each of these thinkers the qualitative difference between merely sensing and having an experience of an external world comes with sensibility, not with reason. We do not infer the existence of an external world from our sensations, they argued: we are aware of its existence by means of a relation to the world that is affective rather than rational. The reasoning behind this is that our knowledge of the world comes through sensation rather than purely through intellectual reflection, and that experience of an external world, as opposed to mere sensation, is prior to having and exercising rational faculties, because these rational faculties are, at least primarily (and for French Lockeans, exclusively), exercised on the basis of our experience of the external world. It follows from this that sensibility not only forms the link between sensation and ratiocination, but it plays a crucial role in what we are and how we think, a role that reason, for example in the form of a faculty that relies on innate ideas, is simply unable to play.

On the move from sensation to experience of the world, consider Condillac's version of the argument. Condillac asks us to imagine a human statue which we bring to life by attributing various sensory faculties to it, one by one. We can separate each stage and ask what its experience of the world would be like at that stage. Imagine we give the statue the power to smell and place a rose in front of its nose, so that the statue experiences the odour of a rose. There is nothing in this experience that would lead the statue to imagine that that experience had an external source, so the olfactory sensation is not experienced as being that of an external object, but simply as an experiential state—and similarly so with the power to hear, to see, to taste. Touch is treated differently by Buffon and Condillac. Buffon argues that the statue at first believes all its sensations to refer to internal experiences, and it is only when a tactile faculty is provided that it realizes, 'in horror', that there is something outside it. Only touch can provide a sense of an external world. Condillac recognized the distinctiveness of tactile sensation, but makes it clear that to gain a general idea of sensation, the statue must reflect on the qualities it senses without reference to the five ways in which the bodies are affecting its organs: that is, it must run together all the individual sensations it receives to form a single class. Nevertheless, even a statue with all five of the senses which was able to compare, reflect, remember, and accomplish the other intellectual operations would not be led, on these grounds alone, to imagine that its states were anything but internal and self-contained. Despite having a grasp of spatial relations, for example, the statue would be solipsistic: its sensory experiences would not project it into, or connect it with, the world. On the contrary, it would remain isolated and self-contained. The question now is, how is it possible for us to develop a conception of the world as independent of us? Buffon's view is that only touch can provide a sense of an external world, and with this sense effectively comes a precondition for morality, in that with it comes a recognition of the existence of others, and a love for them replaces the earlier narcissism. Condillac's answer to the question is that a sense of reflection emerges from the sensations, allowing us to distinguish our own body from the sensations themselves, by combining the sensations and making something new out of them, in which the various objects of sensation can be compared under different descriptions.

For both Buffon and Condillac, sensibility and a recognition of an external world come simultaneously. It is axiomatic to the sensationalist project that one begins life with a blank mind, and the question is how one develops a cognitive, affective, and moral life on this basis. Diderot develops this line of thought most fully, explicitly linking sensation with moral and aesthetic sensibility. He does this through an exploration of the mentality of someone who is deprived of sensory capacities in some way. In his account of blindness in his *Letter on the Blind*, for example, he compares the blind with the sighted in order to explore what this tells us about sensibility in general. A deficient sensibility is primarily a question of an emotional, aesthetic, and moral challenge for Diderot, and because of their impoverished sensibilities, the blind turn their minds inwards and are drawn to thinking in terms of abstractions. The blind offer a crucial case study because he believes that their abstract manner of experiencing pain in others weakens their sense of sympathy for the suffering of others. His target is not confined to the blind, however. The blind just manifest in a particularly concrete way a general insensibility to the world on the part of those who think and experience it in terms of abstractions. For Diderot, our relation to the world depends very much upon how we arrive at that relation, and one assimilates cognitive information in a process which is always and necessarily social, cultural, and has moral implications, so that what is shaped is not merely a cognitive sensibility but a sensibility in which cognitive, affective, and moral questions are inextricably tied together. What is ultimately at stake is the sensory basis of civic life, where the contrast is between sensibility and solipsistic 'rationalism'. The general question underlying this is that of where the ideas that regulate our lives—our moral, emotional, social, political, and intellectual lives—come from. The approach of those metaphysicians and others who conceive of the world in abstract terms, and as a consequence examine our relation to it in these same terms, now becomes not merely misguided but socially and morally irresponsible.

Medical philosophy

In the course of the 18th century, the idea arose that medicine might take over ambitions traditionally fostered in metaphysics and theology, that Hippocrates might replace Socrates, and perhaps even Jesus, as the model for understanding human behaviour. There was the increasing awareness of the place of sensibility in our emotional and cognitive lives, and the belief that medicine might be better placed than philosophy or more traditional forms of physiology to deal with questions of sensibility. As Théophile de Bordeu (1722–76) put it, sensibility 'is most suitable as a basis on which to explain all the phenomena of life, whether in a state of health or of sickness'. As a result,

> this is the way of considering the living body that has been adopted by those who, among modern thinkers, have pursued their speculations beyond practical medicine and the received systems of the schools at the beginning of the century. Such is the scope that philosophical medicine has assumed concerning the purely material functions of the body.

One feature of this medical form of philosophy was that it led to the extension of physiological investigation into the realm of the psychological, and thereby into that of sensation in its fullest sense. This led to the question of the relations between parts and wholes, which had significant consequences not only for how phenomena involving sensibility were examined, but in marking out sensibility from reason, and indeed unifying the epistemological question of sensation and physiological question of sensitivity. With the publication of Condillac's *Essay on the Origin of Human Knowledge* (1746) and *Treatise on Sensation* (1754), there emerged a very influential general account of the whole/parts relation which stood in direct contrast to accounts that assumed the primacy of reason in perceptual cognition, typically through the postulation of innate ideas. Condillac's model was developed to bolster a sensationalist account of perceptual cognition, one in which sensation, rather than reason, was the key to understanding how cognition was possible. Whereas reason had always been construed very much in terms of a single source of rules and procedures regulating our cognitive life, in Condillac's account of sensation we find the inverse of this:

a thoroughly decentralized account of our cognitive life, as reflected in language. Whereas reason encourages a top-down model in which a grasp of the whole is necessary if we are to establish, deductively, a necessary order in the parts, sensibility on this view works in the opposite direction, starting with the parts and building up from these a picture of the whole.

When Condillac took over a Lockean model of perceptual cognition, he radicalized it, rejecting Locke's theory that sensation and reflection were the origins of our ideas, and arguing instead that sensation was the sole source of ideas. This led to a study of the physiology of sensation, and this was followed up in the mid-18th century by physicians based at Montpellier, who expanded it into a medicine of sensibility. In the process, sensation and physiological sensitivity came to be joined up more intimately with the question of moral sensibility, as one's mental life came to be comprehensively medicalized. The relation of the whole to the parts plays a central role here, and Bordeu argued that the whole is as it is because the parts are as they are: in particular, the organism is a living thing because the fibres and organs that make it up are living. The question of the relation between the whole and the parts is now central to the understanding of the nature of life. This bears on one of the most pressing questions in 18th- and 19th-century thought, the nature of life—and the theory that what is 'living' about an organism is its parts, rather than the whole, was a radical one. It contradicted not only Descartes' mechanistic physiology (which had always had problems identifying what it was about living things that distinguished them from the non-living) but also Aristotelian theories whereby life was due to a form suffused throughout the material body.

Bordeu attributes sensibility to all organs, where this sensibility has now become localized: each organ leads a life of its own, and the lives of organs contribute to, indeed constitute, the collective life of the organism. He argues that life is only feeling and movement, and consists of the ability of the animal fibre to feel and to move itself, something that is 'inherent in the primary elements of the living body such as gravity, attraction, and the mobility of various bodies'. In general terms, one might say that it is because the parts are living that the whole is living, and it is because the living parts are connected in the way they are that the whole is the way it is.

The account of life and sensibility proposed here is one in which these qualities exist at a level that is smaller than that of the organism, and in which the smaller organs (or, in the limiting case, simply pieces of organic matter) are autonomous, in that they have these qualities in their own right, not to the extent to which they play some functional role in a hierarchical organization dictated by the needs of the organism. In particular, note that sensibility is a *sine qua non* not only of the autonomy of the organs, but more importantly of the unifying connections that they are able to form. The 'distributed' nature of sensibility, and hence life, is crucial here, because a healthy body is one in which the autonomous parts are in harmony with one another.

In his entry on 'observation' in the *Encyclopedia*, Ménuret spells out the nature of the connections in a famous image:

> one could compare man to a flock of cranes, which fly together in a particular order, without any mutual assistance or dependence on one another. The physicians or philosophers who have studied and carefully observed man have noticed this sympathy in all animal motions: this constant and necessary agreement in the interaction of the various parts, however disparate or distant from one another. They have also noticed the disturbance that results in the whole from the sensible disagreement of a single part. A famous physician (Bordeu) and an illustrious physicist (Maupertuis) likewise compared man, from an illuminating and philosophical point of view, to a swarm of bees that strive together to hang to a branch of a tree. One can see them pressing together and holding one another in place, forming a kind of whole in which each living part

contributes in its way, by the correspondence between and direction of its movements, to sustain this kind of life of the whole body, if we may refer in this way to a mere combination of actions.

A distributive view of life provided a popular model of bottom–up unification for other areas in the 1760s and 1770s. In his *D'Alembert's Dream*, written in 1769, and in the *Elements of Physiology*, published in 1778, Diderot used the model of the unity of the organism to show how there can be a unity of the subject of thought without postulating an immaterial soul. And Rousseau moved effortlessly from the biological version of the question to a political one, asking in *The Social Contract* how an aggregate of individual wills can be transformed into a collective will, and identifying the discovery of a form of government that achieves this as the fundamental problem to which the social contract is a solution.

One consequence of this approach is that the successful conduct of the intellect is now a function of the fibres in the brain. Accordingly, the route to the moral, intellectual, and social life of the individual is a corporeal one, and it works not via reason but via sensibility. In its new expanded domain, however, sensibility no longer looks like something for which physiology or psychology alone could account. Rather it is medicine—a form of medicine in which control of sensibility holds the key—that now becomes the primary tool of investigation. In his influential *The Moral and Physical Idea of Man*, Louis de la Caze (1703–65) explicitly drew out the moral and social consequences of this newly conceived medical science. His starting point is a revival of the doctrine of 'non-naturals', whose first systematic formulation can be traced back to the systematic physician of antiquity Galen (130–201 CE). Factors relating to health are divided there into the naturals, the non-naturals, and the contra-naturals. The naturals were structural and functional elements innate in each body such as the temperaments, humours, parts of the body, faculties, and functions. The non-naturals were those factors that determined the state of the body without being controlled by the natural functioning of the body: ambient air, food and drink, movement or exercise and rest, sleep and waking, excretion and retention, and the passions of the soul. The contra-naturals comprised diseases, and these could result from an internal imbalance in the naturals or from an imbalance between naturals and non-naturals. Health on this account was the result of a proper ordering of the naturals and a proper regimen of the non-naturals, brought under the general notion of 'hygiene'. Since one cannot avoid the effects of the non-naturals, in the Galenic tradition they were included in the curriculum of the medical schools, and physicians were required to learn about them not only to treat diseases but to preserve health and to prevent diseases.

This Galenic conception was revived in 18th-century medicine in France, and there is a shift in the direction of thinking about the role of medicine. The basic medical concern shifted from cure to care, and took on a philosophical significance as a result. It was above all La Caze who set out to establish connections between physiologically characterized sensibility and affective states in terms of a general notion of health as a harmonious 'animal economy'. The crucial thing about this animal economy was that sensations were not just physiological in nature but were pleasurable or painful, with an intensity corresponding to the needs of the animal economy. Our moral habits are determined by this animal economy, in terms of the pleasure or pain with which particular behaviour is associated. But although this means that there is no direct social shaping of behaviour, for example, there is nevertheless an indirect influence, because the 'constitution' of the body, and hence its animal economy, are themselves shaped by the 'constitution' of society, which La Caze argued is variable: regionally, in terms of the social distribution of tasks, and in terms of whether the society is in a savage state, where muscular action is at a premium, or civilized, where sensibility may become too refined. Bordeu's definition of health as harmony and balance comes to be extended to social practice: moderation was the key to health because any kind of excess disturbed bodily harmony. The idea of a harmonious state was generally perceived as a 'natural' state, both in the case of the correct balance of the naturals, and in the case of the balance of the naturals and the non-naturals. The task was that of guiding individuals to the achievement of a natural state. Personal regimen remained the preferred option, and cultivation of sensibility was what this personal regimen involved. But just what the cultivation amounted to was contested. Above all, questions began to be raised about 'the perfectibility of man'.

The issues that are at stake here form the core of disputes in the second half of the 18th century over the extent to which human faculties and behaviour can and should be shaped by social and medical intervention. Beginning in the 1750s, there was a burgeoning stream of literature advocating the use of medicine in these matters, duly accompanied by a number of warnings about the over-stimulation of sensibility. It is in this context that the *médecins philosophes* thrived, for their interests transcended those of traditional medicine and projected it firmly into the moral or human sciences.

With the publication of Rousseau's *Émile, or Education* in 1762, the question of 'the perfectibility of man' was thrust into the forefront of the Republic of Letters. Rousseau, in the imaginary educational experiment to which he subjects Émile in the novel, sets out to show how we might cultivate the kind of sensibility that enables us to act morally. The idea that moral capacities were not equal and were something that could be cultivated was not something new, and indeed it was common ground for generations of thinkers from the late 16th century onwards. Descartes is a case in point. When Descartes dealt with ethical questions in the last decade of his life, in the letters to Princess Elizabeth or in his *Passions of the Soul*, the context was not that of determining which actions were moral and which were not, or whether there was some general principle that we were compelled to follow in genuinely moral judgements. Rather, it was a question of what might be termed a theory of psychological preparation for moral agency: how to reshape one's life so that the anxieties, melancholia, and uncontrolled passions that prevent one taking full control of one's life can be overcome. It is to the degree that one overcomes these, and as a consequence is able to act freely, that one can be said to be a morally responsible agent. Descartes attempted to provide Princess Elizabeth with advice on what to do to transform herself from someone subject to dispersed sensations and affections, with a reduced sense of self, into a unified locus of subjectivity, one that could exercise genuine agency, above all genuine moral agency.

What thinkers such as Diderot and Rousseau rejected in this account was the individualistic solution, as if one could simply reshape one's own psychological resources. In its place they offered a developmental account in which the social and cultural context, especially throughout childhood and adolescence, is crucial for the shaping of sensibility. Rousseau argued that the key to making people virtuous did not lie in training their minds, but in carefully controlling the impressions made upon their bodies, that is, their nervous systems. This is of particular importance in Rousseau's account in *Émile*, because it is the excessive stimulation, the constant excess of impressions, that is the cause of a distorted mode of experiencing and understanding our relations with others. Consequently, one needs to moderate one's exposure to this excess of impressions, by choosing with care one's society, occupations, and pleasures. The sensationalism that drives much of the programme, in Rousseau for example, enables one to include, not just the traditional elements of formal education here, but also the whole social and cultural milieu in which one lives. In short, the cultivation of what French Enlightenment thinkers will refer to as sensibility is quite different from Descartes' cultivation of a sense of the self, in that the source of the problems is located primarily in the social and cultural context in which one is raised, and the impact of excessive stimulation on one's sensibility.

At issue was whether it was simply a matter of increasing one's level of sensibility, or whether one's sensibility could be harmfully over-developed. For many, the cultivation of sensibility was above all a matter of developing one's sensibility to the fullest degree, something seen as crucial to one's formation as a healthy, well-formed, balanced, morally responsive individual. Moreover, since this sensibility is a function of the sensory sources of experience generally, it should in theory be quite possible to control the social and pedagogic environment in such a way as to foster a high degree of sensibility. Of course, not all forms of sensory exposure will have the same effect, and may have different effects in different people. Nevertheless, it was widely considered that many sensory experiences did in fact have a uniform effect: experience of weakness and misery, for example, produced certain affective and emotional states in people.

The fiercest critic of this view was the philosopher-physician Samuel-Auguste Tissot (1728–97), who challenged the assumption of routinely beneficent effects of increasing levels of sensibility. He documents a number of cases where patients have over-taxed themselves in attempting to cultivate sensibility with a view to intellectual and moral development, only to find themselves sick and incapacitated, and constantly agitated. What results is a form of de-sensitization, an effect compounded in the case of exposure to intense cognitive and affective stimulation, and this affects not just the local fibres, but the whole animal economy.

Voltaire and the challenge to the uniqueness of the West

Two distinctive themes in French Enlightenment thought are religion and the superiority of European thought and values, and these are combined in a unique way in Voltaire (1694–1778). His *Essay on Manners* (1756) is a watershed in comparative history. It uses information about China in a way that no other work had done, as a contrast case to identify features of self-conceptions of

Europe, and the historiographical assumptions of its religion, Christianity, that had otherwise escaped attention. Montesquieu (1689–1755) had employed a similar distancing device in the *Persian Letters* (1721), by adopting the persona of a Persian examining and commenting on European society. Voltaire takes the procedure much further. He not only refuses to deploy a Eurocentric model to examine China, but uses China to raise questions about Europe. Here, for the first time, we have a questioning of antiquity and the formative nature of a Euro-Christian understanding of the world.

Like d'Alembert, Voltaire sees Christianity as having acted contrary to reason, having a deleterious effect on the progress of the sciences, and on emancipation, and he is motivated by many of the same concerns as d'Alembert, particularly with countering the Christian historiography that was still shaping thinking about history. His approach is not to attack religion as holding up the progress of knowledge, however, but rather to relativize Christianity: it is one religion among many, and the culture in which it is fostered is one culture among many, certainly not the oldest and noblest, and not something that could ever provide a standard against which other cultures, or other eras, can be judged. For Voltaire, a form of enquiry that integrates historical and geographical perspectives in a coherent way enables us to gain insight into the make-up of societies and cultures by disabusing us of the idea that our parochial values are universal and absolute ones. For Voltaire, the significance of China lies not in a lesson in the extent to which China can be assimilated to the West, as his contemporaries believed, but in the extent to which the West can provide a legitimate framework for understanding China. In particular, the *Essay on Manners* sets out to establish that monotheism is a form of natural religion common to all cultures, contrary to the claims of Judaism and Christianity, which have sought to put highly questionable interpretations on it.

Chapter 4
Post-Revolutionary philosophy: the 19th century and the Third Republic

The Marquis of Condorcet (1743–94) was permanent secretary of the Academy of Sciences, secretary of the French Academy, and the only one of the Enlightenment philosophers to hold office in the Revolutionary government. His commitment to a liberal economy, equal rights for women, and constitutionalism made him the prototype of the Enlightenment thinker. A protégé of d'Alembert, he made contributions to probability theory, and economic and political theory. But his most lasting and best-known contribution was to the idea of progress. Progress was a central concern of Enlightenment thought. D'Alembert, as we have seen, provided a long account of the progress of civilization in the preliminary discourse to the *Encyclopedia*; and Voltaire, in his ruminations on China, had concluded that, while it was an advanced civilization, what China lacked was progress: it was a static form of society. The question then arose what it was about the West that enabled it to progress, and d'Alembert for one had found the answer in science: it was the advance of science, above all, that had broken the dogmatism and sterility of the Middle Ages in his view. Neither developments in the arts nor politics as such could have achieved this because the source of the problem was superstition, and only science has the resources to combat superstition. This became a widely accepted view among French Enlightenment thinkers, but it was Condorcet who, more than anyone else, translated the emphasis on science into the idea of devising a scientific form of political theory. In particular, he proposed a reform of epistemology to encompass collective decision-making, offering a new notion of calculative rationality to replace traditional judgement-based reason.

His *Sketch for a Historical Picture of the Progress of the Human Mind* (1795) offered what was to be a canonical statement of the idea that the inevitability of progress is a basic social-historical law. On Condorcet's account, society proceeds through historical stages towards a goal defined in terms of rationality, manifested in a form of organization of society superior to earlier ones. The early chapters of the *Sketch* offer a conjectural reconstruction of the early history of humanity. It adopts a stadial approach to history, that is, one that sees historical development as progressing through distinct stages. Such a view was developed by the Scottish writers Adam Ferguson (1723–1816) and Dugald Stewart (1753–1828), and in France by Condorcet's mentor Baron Turgot (1727–81). Condorcet's approach is distinctive, however. Rather than tending to treat history as culminating in the present, it is very much future-orientated, seeding 19th-century accounts of history by utopian and socialist writers such as Comte, Marx, and Spencer.

The three early 'epochs' of history in Condorcet's account—formation into 'hordes', formation of pastoral groups, and invention of the alphabet—are those that culminate in the emergence of agricultural society. With the fourth and fifth epochs, those of classical Greece, we encounter the beginnings of science in Pythagoras, whom Condorcet sees as a precursor of Descartes and Newton. Nevertheless, with the rise of science came the rise of the conflict between science and superstition, and the death of Socrates is identified as the 'first crime that the war between philosophy and superstition conceived and brought forth'. After this, there is a decline, first with the Romans, whose eventual military despotism prevented 'the tranquil meditations of philosophy and science' from finding a place, and then, more seriously, with the advent of Christianity, for science threatened its acceptance of miracles and had to be crushed. In short, it is the sciences that offer the strongest defence against superstition, and with the decline of the sciences superstition is renewed, accompanied by an inevitable return to barbarism. Condorcet's association of science and civilization is crucial here, and what connects them is the problem of superstition. Superstition is the obstacle to civilization, and this is something that neither the arts nor the development of good governance, nor the rise of commercial society can offer any resistance to: only science can do that.

The later epochs that Condorcet outlines cover the transition to the modern period, in which the sciences and philosophy threw off the 'Yoke of Authority'. The sciences and civilization are constantly linked, no more so than in the final chapter, the 'tenth epoch', which 'describes the future progress of mankind'. It is clear, we are told, 'from observation of the progress which the sciences and civilization have hitherto made', that 'nature has fixed no limits to our hopes'.

It is science that secures an open-endedness to historical development here. This a novel idea which goes beyond d'Alembert's notion of the present as a culmination of the achievements of the past, for example. The very idea of continuity with the past, assumed as much in d'Alembert's genealogy as in Christian historians, is put in question in the revolutionary programme of the later chapters of the *Sketch*. What drives the move towards the new form of society that Condorcet advocates is not a development in the arts or forms of government as such, but the sciences, including the new science of political economy. As the embodiment of reason, science stands above the events that history describes, providing a prescriptive guidance that enables us to secure not just a freedom from barbarism and superstition, but something unlimited in its potential.

Revolution and reaction

The French Revolution holds a special place in the history of philosophy. For its celebrants and detractors alike, it is the supreme instance of philosophy come to life, not unlike Condillac's statue. The collapse of royal sovereignty in 1789 seemed a vindication of ideas that targeted the authority of religion and tradition, not least those promulgated in Condorcet's 'scientific' understanding of history. Yet as France descended into bloodshed, many were quick to blame philosophy for an attack on inherited norms that seemed to deliver more carnage than political equality.

In a series of writings defending throne and altar, the Savoyard diplomat Joseph de Maistre (1753–1821) came to treat the Revolution as a providential event, divine punishment for the hubris of Enlightenment. With Edmund Burke writing from across the Channel, Maistre became a voice for those troubled by the fate of politics when it is based on reason and abstraction rather than faith and tradition. The thought that we were 'blank slates' on which our philosophical development could be written was part of the problem. Inspired by Malebranche, Maistre was unsubtle in his derision: 'contempt for Locke is the beginning of wisdom'. But here again, Maistre did not negate philosophy of history as such; he offered an alternative, a counter to the progressivism one finds in Condorcet. Later critiques of totalitarianism in the 20th century would occupy a similar stance. Sceptical of any philosophy—be it Rousseau's or Marx's—that purported to know the direction of history, conservatives would repurpose earlier forms of empiricism to suggest history is a piecemeal process, a product of experience and contingencies. Yet to describe history as contingent is no less a philosophical claim than one that deigns to describe its necessities.

The point is that the Enlightenment—and in particular the French Enlightenment—remains central to current conceptions of the relationship between philosophy and politics. The German philosopher Reinhart Koselleck described the French Revolution as ushering in the 'pathogenesis of modernity'. Having established a space of critique outside the political sphere, Enlightenment thinkers inspired revolutionaries to claim a moral high ground that was in some sense 'outside' or 'beyond' politics yet hostile to established religion. The inscrutability of this ground proved to be a problem and licence for all kinds of political misadventures, the basis for Koselleck's metaphor of modernity as a kind of disease. Such is the 'conservative' view. Yet many contemporary historians point to the 'Declaration of the Rights of Man and Citizen' promulgated in 1789 as the foundation of modern human rights. On this view, however bloody it turned out to be in practice, the Enlightenment remains an unfulfilled promise that is still worth pursuing.

One philosopher deeply inspired by French revolutionary politics was none other than Karl Marx (1818–83). The famous eleventh thesis on Feuerbach which states that 'philosophers have heretofore only interpreted the world; the point is to change it' delivers a slogan after the fact for the Enlightenment mythos in its relationship to the French Revolution. But Marx was also inspired by a movement that acquired its name in the wake of the event: socialism. The term was coined by Henri de Saint-Simon (1760–1825) in his efforts to articulate a utopian alternative to the individualism that had run amok in the late 18th century. Saint-Simon inspired many, including the anarchist Pierre-Joseph Proudhon (1809–65), whose most basic idea—that property is theft—would provide a link between Rousseau's theories and Marx's. But arguably the most important of Saint-Simon's many students was one who had a privileged view on the development of his ideas, his secretary Auguste Comte (1798–1857).

Comte

The significance of the French Revolution was Comte's starting point. By contrast with many of his contemporaries, he did not treat the Revolution as an aberration, but as a phenomenon that must be located within a large-scale time line defined by the separation of spiritual and temporal powers. The beginning of the decline and displacement of the former by secular power is traced to the end of the 13th century, and it is here we have the beginnings of 'modern history'. The process finally culminates in the French Revolution. The period associated with the French Revolution, the Enlightenment, was part of what Comte identifies as a transitionary period between that of theology and that of a 'positive' (i.e. scientifically constructed) state. Such a state is the effect, not of Enlightenment ideas as such, but of the advances of science and industry. The Enlightenment ideas associated with these advances, which he terms 'metaphysical', are effective in undermining the theological and monarchical edifice of pre-Revolutionary Europe, but they leave society unbalanced, with no moral authority, and are hence in themselves incapable of effecting the required transition to a new form of balanced society.

Comte's conception of what this balanced society would look like changes radically between his *Course of Positive Philosophy* (1830–42) and his *System of Positive Politics* (1851–4), the former offering a secular conception of the positive society, the latter offering a 'religion of humanity'. The first was immensely influential in the 19th century, whereas the impact of the second was confined to a narrow circle of Comteans, and widely ridiculed elsewhere: the British historian Henry Buckle (1821–62), for example, a staunch advocate of the *Course*, remarked that the *System* contains

> a scheme of polity so monstrously and obviously impracticable, that if it were translated into English, the plain men of our island would lift their eyes in astonishment, and would most likely suggest that the author should for his own sake be immediately confined.

In both cases, however, there was a form of self-reflection that emerged in the final 'positive' stage: 'social physics', as it was initially termed; 'sociology' as it became later. Social physics was explicitly modelled on the other sciences: mathematics, astronomy, physics, chemistry, biology. It emerges through detailed examination of the history and nature of the sciences in the first four books of the *Course*, which are devoted in large part to the question of how each of these disciplines became sciences. From this, Comte derives an account of scientific method, which is then applied to the only area of investigation that has not been subjected to scientific treatment, social physics. The establishment of social physics as a science brings with it a corresponding form of practice, however: it is used to transform politics. Social physics, as an intellectual practice, has a directly transformative effect on the potentialities inherent in social and political life.

For Comte, society was to be reformed on a resolutely scientific basis, and crucial to his project is the ranking of the sciences in order of their fundamental standing: mathematics, astronomy, physics, chemistry, physiology, and 'social physics'. In the final 'positive' stage of social development, social physics, the form of reflection that captures and accompanies the historical development of understanding, offers the one true perspective in which the absoluteness of claims to knowledge can be established. But his extensive account of social physics in volumes V and VI of the *Course* is preceded by volume IV, on chemistry and biology. The biology section is the last of the series on the natural sciences, but it is also in some respects the first on the human sciences. The sequence of societies in volumes V and VI is explicitly grounded in the biological account set out in volume IV. Civilization, for example, is set out in terms that mix historical and biological questions, and comparisons are with animals as much as with primitive social states:

> The influence of civilization in perpetually improving the
> intellectual faculties is even more unquestionable than in its effects
> on moral relations. The development of the individual exhibits to us
> in little, both as to time and degree, the chief phases of social

development. In both cases, the end is to subordinate the satisfaction of the personal instincts to the habitual exercise of the social faculties, subjecting, at the same time, all our passions to rules imposed by an ever-strengthening intelligence, with the view of identifying the individual more and more with the species. In the anatomical view, we should say that the process is to give an influence by exercise to the organs of the cerebral systems, increasing in proportion to their distance from the vertebral column, and their nearness to the frontal region. Such is the ideal type which exhibits the course of human development, in the individual, and, in a higher degree, in the species. This view enables us to discriminate the natural from the artificial part of the process of development; that part being natural which raises the human to a superiority over the animal attributes; and that part being artificial by which any faculty is made to preponderate in proportion to its original weakness: and here we find the scientific explanation of that eternal struggle between our humanity and our animality.

Comte's commitment to providing a scientific basis for his account of humanity was, however, highly selective. He dismissed a number of developments in science on the grounds that they were 'metaphysical'. Cellular theory in biology, for example, reminded him of Leibniz's metaphysical doctrine of monads and so was rejected. Less obviously, he also found sidereal astronomy and probability theory 'metaphysical'. At the same time, in a very revealing move, he was hostile to experimental research because it could lead to awkward discoveries which could result in further uncertainties. Nevertheless, a commitment to a scientific conception of civilization was the core of Comte's project.

Spiritualism

If Comte's project continued the scientific approach to politics and society promoted in Condorcet's account, other 19th-century efforts drew strength from older theological traditions. Little read today, thinkers such as Maine de Biran, Victor Cousin, and Félix Ravaisson came to define the movement known as spiritualism. Historical accounts of 19th-century European philosophy tend to focus on Germany. This is the age, after all, of Kant, Hegel, Marx, and Nietzsche. And a case could be made that these thinkers did more to influence 20th-century French philosophy than any of their Gallic forebears from the same epoch. Nevertheless, it's important to have a sense of spiritualism's significance and its role bridging early and late modern philosophy in France.

Maistre's reaction to the Revolution was accompanied by other Christian apologetics, such as Chateaubriand's *Genius of Christianity* (1802), a stirring defence of the Catholic faith. The work and its author did much to stimulate the Romantic movement in French letters. Like its German counterpart, French Romanticism stressed feeling and sensibility as the sources of the self, rather than abstract rationality. Spiritualism gave romanticism a theological cast by finding in the sensible self an entity beyond description in the law-like regularities of science.

In philosophy, 19th-century spiritualism began with Maine de Biran (1766–1824). Originally an empiricist who thought in ways close to Condillac and Locke, Maine de Biran later came to stress the importance of will. But in the final stage of his career, once he had reconciled with the Church, he advanced a form of mystical theosophy in which the inner life of man is in a kind of unity with God via the mechanisms of divine grace. In this development, we see again the resumption of certain Malebranchist ideas. Unable to unify the distinct spheres of Cartesian substance, mind and matter, Malebranche was happy to ground this unity in God himself, that figure in whom 'we live and move and have our being' (Acts 17:28). Maine de Biran offered a resolution that was similarly persuasive to thinkers who did not share his religious convictions.

One philosopher persuaded by at least some of Maine de Biran's views was Victor Cousin (1792–1867), a figure who was to have a towering importance for the development of education in 19th-century France as the Minister of Public Instruction during the July Monarchy. The nationalization of education with philosophy at its pinnacle is recognizable today to anyone acquainted with French schooling. It has its roots in Cousin's efforts.

As for his ideas, Cousin was notable for developing the spiritualist tendencies of Maine de Biran—whose writings he posthumously edited—in dialogue with the legacy of German Idealism. Like Kant, Cousin believed that philosophical enquiry began with psychology, but only as a means to arrive at conclusions of a more fundamental variety. He demurred from the consequence of the Kantian project in Hegel, seeing in the latter's doctrine of Absolute Being an abstraction. The locus of being for Cousin remained within consciousness and its ground in sensation. This is how a focus on sensibility gives way to spiritualism. That which is deemed beyond representation, to the extent that it is beyond concepts and scientific manipulation, is deemed to be metaphysically fundamental. Hegel saw Spirit in World History. Cousin didn't *see* 'spirit' at all. It was the ground of experience, making all forms of vision possible.

Cousin is also associated with 'eclecticism' in philosophy. He borrowed so much from a range of contemporaries and precursors that it is hard to specify his unique contribution. Yet his influence was felt throughout the remainder of the 19th century, not least via his student Félix Ravaisson (1813–1900). Less eclectic than his mentor—whom he criticized on this score—Ravaisson is best remembered for his short book *Of Habit*, first published in 1838. The book finds in the repetitions of habit an entrée to a metaphysics of nature, one that also drew inspiration from another of Ravaisson's teachers: F. J. W. Schelling. For a thinker like Hume, a turn to habit had been a way to undermine metaphysics, replacing putatively necessary relationships with contingent sequences. For Ravaisson, habit was itself a metaphysical crossroads, the site of unity between consciousness and nature. Twentieth-century thinkers from Heidegger to Deleuze would likewise find in 'mindless' repetition new ways to think about the ontological foundations of mind.

Today, if these thinkers are read at all, they are read as precursors, a category that provokes the scepticism of historians. Whatever its claim on us, the development of spiritualism in the 19th century complicates self-congratulatory stories on the part of 'enlightened' or scientific philosophers committed to a progressivist view of French philosophy premised on the rejection of religion.

Philosophy in the Third Republic: Brunschvicg and Bergson

Comte's positivism was emblematic for French social thought in the Third Republic (1871–1940). Born from French defeat at the hands of the Germans, and reeling from the violence of the Paris Commune, the Third Republic saw a growing nationalist element to French philosophy. Whatever was German was to be treated with scepticism if not contempt; whatever the glories of idealism, militarism was the result. Local traditions were paramount. Comte's science of society inspired the sociology of Émile Durkheim (1858–1916), which treated society as an organic totality describable in terms of 'social facts'. The positivist injunction to attend solely to the data themselves, and to prohibit grand or speculative metaphysical inferences, permeated culture. Impressionist painting by Claude Monet looks blurry to non-initiates; but the technique was positivistic insofar as Monet painted precisely what he saw, and what he saw changed and shifted according to light and perspective. Likewise, the novels of Émile Zola limited themselves to descriptions without judgement, refusing to find fault in characters whose behaviour was caused by their environments and histories. This 'naturalism' disclosed society as it was, not as we might wish it to be. The literary genre was continuous with Comte's project in that respect.

More than a novelist, Zola acquired even greater fame with 'J'Accuse!', his 1898 newspaper articled condemning the hypocrisies of the Dreyfus Affair. The anti-Semitism in play in the trial of Colonel Alfred Dreyfus—charged with treason and espionage on behalf of the Germans—was contrary to the egalitarian spirit of the Republic. If Enlightenment philosophers helped to forge a public sphere outside state power, Zola continued the tradition and was also the first to embody the 20th-century figure of the intellectual. Lacking political authority, Zola nevertheless spoke for the values of an ideal republic failing to live up to its promises. Thinkers on the right who disagreed with Zola, such as Maurice Barrès, coined the term 'intellectuals' as a pejorative for those who relied on their abstractions to question state power.

One consequence of the Affair was to further embed republican values in the higher education system. Among the Dreyfusards was the philosopher and leading light of French neo-Kantianism or 'critical idealism', Léon Brunschvicg (1869–1944). With Xavier Léon and Élie Halévy, Brunschvicg founded in 1893 the *Revue de métaphysique et de morale*, a journal which remains one of the most esteemed in the discipline of philosophy in France to this day. Several years later he formed the *Société française de la philosophie*, still a major arbiter of the profession in Paris. From 1909 he was stationed at the Sorbonne, where he would shape the curriculum nationwide via his influence on the baccalaureate and the *agrégation* exam, the test which aspiring philosophy teachers must pass to pursue their careers in France.

Deeply hostile to German Idealism—he once claimed that Hegel had 'the mental age of a twelve-year-old'—Brunschvicg had no problem borrowing heavily from Kant to write a series of works celebrating the progressive nature of scientific and philosophical history, works that served to vindicate the Third Republic as a political and cultural entity. His first study, *The Modality of Judgement* (1893), formed a bridge between spiritualism and a more epistemologically oriented neo-Kantianism. *The Stages of Mathematical Philosophy* (1912) was a sweeping history of mathematics that would inspire 20th-century efforts in the history of science from the interwar years up through the 'archaeological' approach to the sciences promoted by Michel Foucault. With reason, many credit the arrival of German phenomenology with shaping French philosophy of science. But Brunschvicg's focus on the integrated nature of scientific theory and practice in history—supremely evident in his 1922 study *Human Experience and Physical Causality*—laid the ground for much of this French work.

His final major work tried to do for the history of morality what previous books had done for mathematics and physics. But in the wake of the First World War and the existential and political crises it unleashed, Brunschvicg's optimistic vision had trouble getting new recruits. In 1932, a young Paul Nizan published *The Watchdogs*, a Marxist broadside that singled out Brunschvicg as a bourgeois apologist whose idealism was easily subverted by a 'materialist' philosophy. Nizan's friend Jean-Paul Sartre would engage further with Marxism in order to undermine the philosophical justifications for the Third Republic offered in Brunschvicg's work. Despite his towering importance and influence, Brunschvicg is little read today. A secular Jew, he survived the Fall of France, dying in internal exile in Aix-en-Provence in 1944.

With its integrative focus on the sciences, Brunschvicg's work was formative for French structuralism, even if that influence has largely been erased by a generation of thinkers who willed themselves into being by insisting on a break with past philosophy. Here the neo-Kantian element was central. Paul Ricoeur once described Claude Lévi-Strauss's structural anthropology as

'Kantianism without a transcendental subject'. A similar description might apply to Foucault's efforts to uncover a 'historical a priori' that provided intelligibility to the history of the sciences. Brunschvicg relied on Kant to combat psychologism and the ahistorical abstractions of logical positivism. And as noted he had no patience for talk of World Spirit. The intelligibility of scientific history drew from a unity internal to that history itself. Sympathetic students such as Jean Cavaillès would find Brunschvicg to be still too captive to the importance of biography in scientific and philosophical history. But they would develop the structural kernel of his thought in other directions, to be explored further in Chapter 5.

Besides psychology and logical positivism, the other great philosophical nemesis for Brunschvicg was spiritualism, especially in its latest form: the process philosophy of Henri Bergson (1859–1941). At first glance, it might seem strange to regard Bergson as an inheritor of spiritualism. His most famous coinage was the *élan vital*, the concept which represented that unrepresentable substrate of experience and duration that our mental faculty captured and fixed in concepts and images. The term suggests why Bergson is often regarded as a 'vitalist', alongside other philosophers of life such as Nietzsche and Dilthey. But clearly the opposition between life and spirit was a false one for Bergson. Much of his work was given to recovering those aspects of existence that an obsession with spatial representation, descending from Descartes, had obscured.

Premised on a rejection of mechanism that he saw resurgent in positivist social science and its neo-Kantian avatars in philosophy, Bergson's philosophy quickly captured the public imagination in France at the *fin de siècle*. His first book, *Essai sur les données immédiates de la conscience* (1889, translated as *Time and Free Will*), sought to solve the dilemma of compatibilism by stipulating that the problem of freedom's relationship to physical determinism was poorly posed. Attention to immediate experience would show that the world was not static and fixed with movements according to laws, but rather a distended experience of temporal duration. Theories of perception from Descartes and Locke aimed to understand how data coming in via our senses managed to fit with the forms of representation encoded in our minds. Bergson changed the picture by focusing on the qualitative intensity of duration; there is no problem of fit between inside and outside because there is only a single process rooted in the temporal unity between mind and world.

Bergson's next book, *Matter and Memory* (1896), developed these ideas further. Inspired by Ravaisson on habit, Bergson found in memory a locus for the union of mind and world proposed in his first book. When we perceive data, its form comes not from transcendental features of mind, such as Kant proposed, but from the totality of accreted images which our memory comprises. We come to recognize things because of repetition. If the affect seems far from Hume's sober empiricism on this score, the proximity of the view, *contra* various forms of idealism, should be clear. It's not for nothing that Bergson's ideas appealed to the American pragmatist William James. Likewise, Gilles Deleuze would later link Bergson with Hume as progenitors of a peculiar form of 'transcendental empiricism'.

Bergson's rhetoric and reliance on notions of intuition and 'qualitative intensity' resonated with the public, but also accounted for the antipathy towards his work in analytic philosophy, then ascendant in the Anglophone world. An acolyte of Bertrand Russell's and important philosopher of mind in his own right, Gilbert Ryle once remarked that trying to explain life by appeal to an *élan vital* was akin to explaining the operations of a train by appeal to an *élan locomotive*. The example is timely, but the critical device dates back to Leibniz and his analogy of the mind as a mill. No matter how fine-grained or small one's scale becomes, you can't find the millworker running things inside the head. Bergson for his own part didn't see his notion of the *élan vital*—

given its most expansive expression in his most popular work, *Creative Evolution* (1907)—as an instance of the homunculus problem but as a resolution to it. The problem with epistemology and philosophies of mind is that they kept looking for the guarantors of knowledge inside the head. In Bergson's picture, there was no inside or outside, but again a singular process.

Bergson quickly garnered acclaim. By 1896 he was teaching at the Collège de France. His lectures there would inadvertently play a role in the Catholic revival in France, inspiring Jacques Maritain (1882–1973) and his wife Raïssa in their conversion to the faith. Though Maritain would go on to write a condemnation of Bergson's philosophy, the integralist nature of his own later doctrine of personalism would be fundamental to the doctrine of human rights that he penned during the Second World War and which inspired the United Nations Charter. Also a secular Jew, Bergson would come close to Catholic mystical themes, especially in his final work, *The Two Sources of Morality and Religion* (1932), but he stopped short of conversion.

Oxford gave Bergson an honorary doctorate in 1909, and in 1914 he was elected to the Académie Française. He was the Nobel Laureate in Literature for 1930, something of a poisoned chalice for a philosopher, seeing that the cause for celebration was his work's literary qualities rather than its truth value (though, n.b., Bertrand Russell won the same award in 1950). Many developments contributed to the eclipse of Bergson's significance. His philosophy of time made for some ill-advised commentary on Einstein's theory of relativity. His increasing mysticism was no more appealing than Brunschvicg's idealism to a generation keen to find new philosophical resources. Heidegger contributed to the derision by repeatedly using the Bergsonian doctrine of intuition as a foil for his own more 'fundamental ontology' in *Being and Time* (1927). 'Time' had been essential to Bergson's brand, but a new authority captured the hearts and minds of French thinkers on this score.

Recent years have seen a Bergson revival due largely to Gilles Deleuze's work and also an increasing historical appreciation for Bergson's role in stimulating developments in phenomenology from Maurice Merleau-Ponty to Emmanuel Levinas. Not for nothing did the latter describe the arrival of phenomenology as the advent of 'True Bergsonianism'. What this suggests is there are as many continuities as breaks in the historical development of French philosophy. Phenomenology's place in this story will occupy our attention in Chapter 5.

Chapter 5
Philosophy in wartime: phenomenology and existentialism

Shortly after Michel Foucault's death in 1984, the *Revue de métaphysique et de morale* published a piece entitled 'Life: Experience and Science'. Originally written as an introduction to the English translation of Georges Canguilhem's study of medical concepts, *The Normal and the Pathological*, the essay contained Foucault's reflections on French philosophy in a broad sense. At the heart of his account was a schematic opposition, one that has been regularly deployed since to describe the conflicts shaping modern French thought. Whatever the disagreements between Marxists and non-Marxists or the different opinions on the value of psychoanalysis, Foucault saw a 'dividing line' running through the century, cross-cutting them all:

> It is one that separates a philosophy of experience, of meaning, of the subject, and a philosophy of knowledge, of rationality, and of the concept. On one side, a filiation which is that of Jean-Paul Sartre and Maurice Merleau-Ponty; and then another, which is that of Jean Cavaillès, Gaston Bachelard, Alexandre Koyré and Canguilhem.

To be sure, Foucault noted the deeper roots of this division in the 19th century, for example in the divergent traditions emanating from Maine de Biran and Comte. And others have repurposed Foucault's heuristic to great effect. In his 2006 treatise *Logics of Worlds*, Alain Badiou situated his proclivity for mathematics in a legacy stemming from Brunschvicg rather than Bergson. Around the same time, the great historian of French psychoanalysis Elisabeth Roudinesco said we might do better to think of Foucault's distinction as one between Cartesians and Spinozists. That the Cartesian side would come to stand for that of experience and meaning rather than the rationality of the concept is one of the peculiar twists of this story. It finds at least part of its explanation in arguably the defining intellectual event of the interwar years: the arrival of German phenomenology in the French encounter with the works of Edmund Husserl and Martin Heidegger.

The revisions to Foucault's opposition have obscured the specificity of his claim: that the division of 20th-century French philosophy—notwithstanding antecedents—had its sources in the conflicting responses to phenomenology and its epochal significance. Thinkers like Sartre and Merleau-Ponty were initially inspired by Husserl, but quickly came to be gripped by Heidegger's existential brand of phenomenology. The philosophers of science on the other side of the pole pursued the logical and formalist sides of Husserl's effort—more specifically, the effort to articulate an ontology that would ground rather than undermine scientific rationality, as Heidegger's work threatened to do. When Husserl introduced phenomenology to a French audience in Paris in 1929, he entitled his lectures 'Cartesian Meditations'. The choice was flattering to his hosts, but also communicated the breadth of Husserl's own self-regard. He saw phenomenology as reinvigorating the fundamental movement of modern philosophy. Apparently Merleau-Ponty followed along in rapt attention, even though he didn't speak German. Cavaillès was also in attendance and was led to believe that phenomenology might contain resources for providing a philosophical basis to mathematical set theory.

The arrival of this new form of thought converged with the rediscovery of a German giant from the previous century:

G. W. F. Hegel. For years derided as an apologist for militarism, Hegel became enlisted alongside Husserl and Heidegger as a thinker of existence and an antidote to both the anaemic neo-Kantianism of Brunschvicg and the Romantic vitalism of Bergson. Here the central figure was Alexandre Kojève, a Russian émigré who had studied phenomenology in Berlin before arriving in Paris. In the 1930s, Kojève gave a series of lectures at the École Pratique des Hautes Études on Hegel's *Phenomenology of Spirit* that were attended by the burgeoning intellectuals of the age: Sartre, Merleau-Ponty, and Simone de Beauvoir, but also Jacques Lacan, Georges Bataille, and the novelist Raymond Queneau, who would edit Kojève's lectures for publication. The central focus of the course concerned the dialectic between 'master' and 'slave' at the heart of Hegel's philosophical anthropology. Filtering Hegel through a Heideggerian prism, Kojève saw history as a struggle for recognition that took the form—sometimes literally, otherwise metaphorically, but in all cases ubiquitously—as a fight to the death.

In this vision, the slave would ultimately have the upper hand because of his knowledge of his dependence on the master for his existence. The master's blindness to his own dependence on the slave, a kind of ignorance, would prove to be his downfall. This sense of struggle, and the notion that the oppressed would have their day per the laws of history, galvanized a generation impatient with the idealism of the Third Republic and faced with a political crisis defined by the extremes of Communism and Fascism. Yet there is irony in Kojève's celebrity. The same lectures that inspired intellectuals with the notion that history might be decoded also put forth the notion that history had in effect ended with the French Revolution and Napoleon. The editor of the English translation of Kojève's lectures, Allan Bloom, would be a right-wing stalwart in the American Culture Wars of the 1980s. In his view, Kojève's lectures paint 'a powerful picture of our problems as those of post-historical man with none of the classic tasks of history to perform, living in a universal, homogeneous state where there is virtual agreement on all the fundamental principles of science, politics, and religion'. It might not be coincidental that Kojève's postwar career would see him working as an intellectual functionary for the European Economic Community, forerunner to the European Union.

In his classic account of 20th-century French philosophy, published prior to Foucault's essay, in 1979, Vincent Descombes described the moment of existentialism that emerged in the interwar years as one dominated by the 'three H's'—Hegel, Husserl, and Heidegger. In Descombes's optic, we can account for the movement from existentialism to the structuralism (and poststructuralism) of the 1960s and 1970s as a transition away from the 'H's' to the three 'masters of suspicion': Marx, Nietzsche, and Freud. One can now quibble with the details. Heidegger was equally significant to existentialists and post-structuralists; Freud's reception began before the Second World War. But Descombes's framework remains plausible; it is not so much an alternative to Foucault's schema as a complement to it.

Our task in this chapter and Chapter 6 is to present the developments in French philosophy with the assistance of these two heuristics. The years surrounding the Second World War were undoubtedly those in which existentialist themes dominated. Yet the structuralist critique of existentialism that emerged in the 1960s did not spring from nowhere. Its antecedents also lay in the interwar years, in the very same reception history of phenomenology that helped shape French existentialism. An indication of both the significance of this reception and certain of its contingent features can be gleaned from considering the more concrete history of specific texts.

For example, we've mentioned Heidegger's significance in this period. But what did Heidegger mean to French readers? He didn't lecture in Paris as Husserl did and his personal contacts were few. Kojève, along with the writings and teachings of his patron and fellow émigré Alexandre Koyré, had helped disseminate Heideggerian ideas. But the first translations came from a student in attendance at Kojève's lectures, Henry Corbin, later the French (and a world-renowned) authority on Islamic philosophy. In 1931, Corbin published translations of Heidegger's 1929 texts *What is Metaphysics?* and *On the Essence of Ground*. These were combined in a volume in 1938 with further translations, also by Corbin, of the introduction to *Being and Time* and large portions of Heidegger's book on Kant. The themes of these selections—above all the notions of a quest for an ever elusive ground to philosophical thought and an end to metaphysics—set the terms for much of the French philosophy to come. More significant in the short term were some of Corbin's translation choices. Most notoriously, he rendered *Dasein*—the keyword of *Being and Time*, which translates literally as 'there-being' or 'being-there' and purports to describe the distinctive ontological feature of humans, those beings for whom being is in question—as *réalité humaine*, that is, 'human reality'. This choice would shape Sartre's humanist appropriation of Heidegger and come in for criticism later when Heidegger enjoyed prestige as a source of anti-humanism for thinkers such as Derrida and Foucault. The translation is not 'wrong' of course—one interpreter's inspired rendering is another's mistranslation. But the case is indicative of the role that contextually specific choices can play in giving the history of philosophy, even recent philosophy, its intelligibility.

The remainder of this chapter will look first at the leading lights of the age: Jean-Paul Sartre, Simone de Beauvoir, and Maurice Merleau-Ponty. The final section will consider what was significant about French epistemology after phenomenology's arrival, those 'philosophers of the concept' that Foucault deemed opposed to the primacy accorded to experience, meaning, and the subject. The focus will be on the philosophical claims and positions, but the political context must be borne in mind here. Even if 'existentialism' doesn't seem like a viable option in academic philosophy today, French or otherwise, its capacity to capture the attention of readers, particularly youthful ones, remains vibrant. Much of the pathos of existentialism comes from its direct confrontation with questions of life and death. Sartre's and Merleau-Ponty's philosophical masterpieces were published in 1943 and 1945 respectively, during the climax of the Second World War. Hence it must be recalled that existence was a pressing, daily matter for Europeans in the first half of the 20th century.

Sartre and Beauvoir

Arguably the greatest philosopher of 20th-century France was Jean-Paul Sartre (1905–80). He's certainly the one who achieved the greatest renown. Not only did he win the Nobel Prize for Literature, he refused it, contemptuous of its tendency to turn writers into institutions. An accomplished novelist and playwright, he also produced a series of major philosophical works that served to define existentialism for readers worldwide. Drawing on 19th-century authors such as Kierkegaard, Nietzsche, and Dostoevsky, Sartre integrated an outlook in which existence was devoid of any pre-given meaning with a recondite philosophical methodology drawn from Husserl. It's been debated how well Sartre understood Heidegger, and even to what extent he cared for Heidegger's work. Per Heidegger's own account in his 'Letter on Humanism', which appeared shortly after Sartre's widely publicized 1945 lecture 'Existentialism is a Humanism', not very well. But there is no doubt about Sartre's enthusiasm for phenomenology. Legend has it that shortly after his friend Raymond Aron explained to him that there was a new German movement that would allow you to make philosophy out of your experience of a cocktail glass, he rushed to the bookstore to purchase Emmanuel Levinas's book on Husserl and started reading it before the pages were cut.

Existentialist themes run through Sartre's writings. His novel *Nausea* (1938) follows the writer Antoine Rocquentin around

Bouville ('Mudville'—a stand-in for Le Havre, where Sartre was teaching high school) as he becomes increasingly disgusted by the thingly qualities of the objects and nature around him. *The Roads to Freedom* (1945–9) was a trilogy of novels in which Sartre reckoned with the fall of France and the political shame it generated for a republic that had lost its way. Among other things we see in these fictions the playing out of the central thesis of his most significant philosophical treatise *Being and Nothingness* (1943): that *existence precedes essence*.

If we take a long view on the history of philosophy, the notion that essence precedes existence seems to be a given. In a Platonist outlook, things that exist are instances of essences that are ontologically prior to them or at any rate independent of them. The essence of chairness is in some sense prior to all the existing chairs. How can you recognize a chair if you don't know what a chair is? You can see how this framework can accommodate a Christian outlook. The essence of man—his soul—is prior to or at any rate independent of the concrete existing man. God precedes the world. In fact, God is the only entity for which it is the case that essence and existence perfectly coincide.

The priority given to essence survived the Cartesian revolution in philosophy. The *cogito* as the essence of one's self is certainly deemed prior to the body, at least to the extent that its creation by God is independent of the material causes that produced one's body. With the challenges to faith in a creator-God growing over the centuries, such a view became harder to sustain. What if the world is simply given as it is, and nothing more? What if it really is 'full of sound and fury', yet 'signifying nothing'?

These themes—coalescing in a tendency towards nihilism over the course of the 19th century—were what Sartre repurposed with phenomenology in a provocative philosophy of freedom. Kierkegaard counselled that in a world devoid of significance, a meaning for one's actions could be achieved only with a leap of

faith. Shorn of the theological element, this would become the
Sartrean political doctrine of commitment. The world will not tell
you what is right; you must choose. Nietzsche's reckoning with the
nihilistic outcome of European history led to similar desires to
forge a new theory of creation *ex nihilo*.

Such themes were far from Husserl's original concerns. He
promoted phenomenology as a method that avoided the traps of
empiricism and rationalism. The method is pursued in the first
instance by suspending our 'natural attitude', an attitude which
leads us to believe we have direct perceptual access to the objects
surrounding us. The goal is to redirect our attention to the forms
of appearance themselves. The ambiguity of phenomenology was
to the point for Husserl, precisely because the relationship
between a thing that appears and the fact of its appearance is
ambiguous.

Yet how is it that the world appears to us at all? Such was Kant's
question as well, which resulted in his philosophy of
transcendental idealism. Husserl thought that pursuing this
question in a more rigorous way would lead not to idealism, but
instead would put us in touch with essences themselves. When I
regard the green leaf, if I bracket out every particular of the
perception, I should find myself left with a perception of
greenness itself—the essence (or *eidos*) of green.

Sartre radicalized Husserl's approach. For in the end no matter
how deeply one 'reduces' one's experience—however far one
carries out the 'phenomenological reduction'—there is always
farther to go. In other words, the essences we find are never
simply given as they are. When I arrive at the perception of
greenness, why not keep going and ask after the form of that
appearance? All that seems to be given, ultimately, is the fact of
existence itself. In some sense, this sounds like Descartes'
cogito—hence, Husserl's 'Cartesian Meditations'. But it also points
to Sartre's repurposing of this tradition. The *fact* of the *cogito* is

without content; it's a mere form. When we reduce and reduce to try to perceive the essence of consciousness, we perceive that there is nothing there, its content always seems to come from elsewhere. The existence of consciousness precedes its essence.

The subtitle of *Being and Nothingness* is 'An Essay on Phenomenological Ontology'. In Sartre's understanding, the phenomenological method ultimately shows that there are only two kinds of beings in the world. There's the whole world of matter, objects, things. Each of these things is a 'being-in-itself'. It is in some sense complete, the product of natural causes and nothing more—the malformed root of the oak tree that provokes Roquentin's disgust. By contrast, our consciousness, our awareness, is a 'being-for-itself', incomplete, and always defined by its projects. (Think of the word 'project' in 'projectile'—whatever we plan to do, all action, is a kind of projection out into the world.) But in Sartre's analysis, what we find when we pursue a phenomenological description of that 'being-for-itself' is that there is no being there to be described. The title of Sartre's work—*L'Être et le néant*—gains something in English translation, for 'nothingness' suggests the notion of 'no-thingness', the lacking of any thing-like quality. Whatever the *cogito* is, it can't be isolated and described as an essence that is wholly 'in itself'.

This lack of essence in consciousness is intimately linked to our freedom. For Rousseau, the trappings of civilization had put humans everywhere in chains. The result was that one ought to be 'forced to be free'. For Sartre one need not be forced to be free for we are all 'condemned to be free'. Such is our 'situation', a keyword that provided the title to Sartre's multiple volumes of occasional writings on politics and the arts. We always find ourselves in a situation and our choices are always relative to a situation. All freedom, all decisions are bound by a situation, which is itself composed of the recalcitrant world of objects: beings-in-themselves.

In this regard, the relationship between 'being' and 'nothingness' might seem fairly straightforward. Where things get complicated is in the relationship with others. How does one nothingness encounter another nothingness? In his play *No Exit* (1944) Sartre's mouthpiece concludes 'Hell is other people'. Others are a restriction on our freedom. They appear as objects but they also place demands on us, and their gaze makes us objects in turn.

A famous scene in *Being and Nothingness* expresses these dilemmas well. In a discussion of 'bad faith', Sartre portrays the café waiter who is a little too perfect in his mannerisms as a waiter. The waiter is in bad faith insofar as he conforms too readily to a role. He makes an object of himself and thereby denies his freedom. This notion that a loss of freedom and life attends to the routinization of our action is incidentally one common to Bergson and Sartre, pointing to a continuity across the phenomenological caesura. But the real ingenuity of Sartre's analysis of bad faith—and what gives his phenomenology its existential twist—is in his showing that its putative opposite, sincerity, is also an instance of bad faith. For when we believe ourselves sincere, we dupe ourselves into believing that we couldn't think or be otherwise in our comportment. That's what makes it sincerity. But to do that is to deny one's freedom. Sincerity is the ultimate act of bad faith. This comes out in Sartre's discussion of the 'homosexual' and the friend who inveighs upon him to admit his identity, in effect to be honest and sincere and without shame about who he is. But in Sartre's reading, such a conforming to a category would be to deny one's freedom no less than failing to admit to the consequences of one's actions. To predicate one's identity—to avow 'I am X' whatever X is—is to allow oneself to be objectified.

Sartre's writing would become increasingly politicized. Never a Communist Party member, he considered himself a 'fellow-traveller' to anti-capitalism. He also lent his authority to the anti-colonial struggles that rocked France throughout the post-war decades, for example in writing the preface to *The Wretched of the Earth*, a vital text in the history of anti-colonialism and *Négritude* written by the psychiatrist and revolutionary from Martinique, Frantz Fanon (1925–61). And perhaps the greatest political significance for nominally Sartrean themes is found not in a book by Sartre at all.

Simone de Beauvoir's *The Second Sex* (1949) is one of the central works of modern feminism. In this book, Beauvoir famously claimed that 'one is not born, but rather becomes, a woman'. This phrase gathers several threads of argument. On the one hand, Beauvoir means to suggest that there is no 'essence' of Woman prior to or independent of the existence of women. In this sense, the category of women has an existence apart from any essence. On the other hand, Beauvoir means to track all the ways in which the category of 'Woman' is constructed as if it were an essence, and how then this essence is foisted upon women. Women comprise 'the second sex' because the entire historical discourse of womanhood and femininity is derivative of 'the first sex'—man. The book itself comprises two halves. In the first part, devoted to 'myths', Beauvoir explores all the ways thinkers have sought to explain and portray women; the second part focuses on experiences of women themselves. In all cases, the category is constructed, the essence is to be provided—either imposed on women from without, or generated by women themselves.

Various ambiguities run through Beauvoir's existentialist brand of feminism, not least in the potential conflict between an approach that focuses on the individual and the meaning-making quality of her choices and actions and a commitment all the same to the reality of a group identity that obtains across time. We can see the lingering effects of Kojève's Hegelianism as an anthropological account of struggle in Beauvoir's take on the apparent contradiction between history and biological necessity in the case of women's oppression:

The bond that unites her to her oppressors is not comparable to any other. The division of the sexes is a biological fact, not an event in human history. Male and female stand opposed within a primordial *Mitsein* [being-with, or being-together], and woman has not broken it. The couple is a fundamental unity with its two halves riveted together, and the cleavage of society along the line of sex is impossible. Here is to be found the basic trait of woman: she is the Other in a totality of which the two components are necessary to one another.

In a global context, Beauvoir is typically associated with 'second-wave feminism'. If the first wave sought equal rights for women, the second wave insisted on the real distinction between the sexes and the need for women to create an identity independent of that yielded by a history dominated by men, in effect, to cease being 'the Other'. But anticipations of 'third-wave feminism' are already evident in Beauvoir's work, for example in her insistence on a tension between a gendered conception of 'woman' as an array of practices and attitudes lacking any original essence, and the 'biological fact' of sexual difference. For Beauvoir the reality of sexual difference is of existential significance precisely in the complications it creates for any notion of generic human essence.

The Second Sex was Beauvoir's greatest theoretical work, but her numerous fictions and memoirs are essential to our understanding of 20th-century French philosophy. In her writing she was typically deferential to Sartre, treating her own work as derivative of his. But there is no doubt about her contribution to his intellectual development. They formed one of the truly great enduring intellectual partnerships of modern European thought. Few stood by Sartre's side otherwise. His fellow existentialist Albert Camus broke with him over Algeria, with Sartre endorsing the radical measures of the Front Libération Nationale. When pressed on his failure to support violent anti-colonial struggle in northern Africa, Camus, born in Algiers, conceded that between justice and his mother, he would choose his mother. Others were troubled by Sartre's increasing commitment to Marxism, which he ultimately identified as 'the unsurpassable horizon of our time'. Sartre's fidelity to the project in the East raised the ire of Camus and Aron, but also Merleau-Ponty, who came to castigate Sartre for his 'ultra-Bolshevism' in his own reckoning with the consequences of Stalinism in *Adventures of the Dialectic* (1955).

Merleau-Ponty

If Sartre is the most famous French phenomenologist, Maurice Merleau-Ponty (1908–61) has a strong case to be considered the most philosophically significant of the period, the one whose project continues to inform a variety of research programmes today. Part of this stems from Merleau-Ponty's longstanding engagement with psychology and a burgeoning cognitive science. True to the Cartesian tradition, Merleau-Ponty's approach to philosophy was not hostile to science. Also true to the Cartesian tradition was Merleau-Ponty's focus on the 'mind–body' problem, the primary concern evident in his major studies, *The Structure of Behaviour* (1942), *The Phenomenology of Perception* (1945), and *The Visible and the Invisible* (1964), the last of which was unfinished at the time of his death.

Foucault placed Merleau-Ponty as a thinker of experience and the subject alongside Sartre. To be sure, experience was a central category in Merleau-Ponty's thought. He may have been inspired by Descartes and the renewal of his project in Husserl's phenomenology, but Merleau-Ponty was no dualist. One of his central arguments was that any attempt to separate mind and body, rather than regard them as a unitary ground of experience, was bound to fail. He was sustained in this by empirical research stemming from the First World War into the fate of the wounded. Against a positivistic behaviourism, Merleau-Ponty took a holistic approach that regarded the body as a mediating vector of environmental factors. Stimulated by the work of the German physiologist Kurt Goldstein, Merleau-Ponty thought that the structure of this holistic field might be described phenomenologically. When combined with his interest in the structural linguistics of Ferdinand de Saussure, this focus on structure in Merleau-Ponty's earliest major work complicates a story in which we regard structuralism as having come along to displace phenomenology. Structural concerns were a unifying theme of Merleau-Ponty's effort up to his premature death from a stroke in 1961, when he was in his prime, lecturing at the Collège de France.

Merleau-Ponty's greatest work was *The Phenomenology of Perception.* Here was elaborated at length an alternative to an empiricist tradition that regards perception as a matter of combining various 'sense-data' into objects of attention. The great quandary of empiricism had always been how a sequence of physical causes—light from one source (an object) impinging on another (the eye)—gets converted into an actual perception, a conscious idea. Presumably light travels elsewhere in the physical universe with no perception taking place. In Merleau-Ponty's view, this picture is totally misguided, as it is as well in an intellectualist or rationalist view that treats mind as a unique substance capable of synthesizing perceptions from raw data. The body, up to and including the eye, is not distinct from mind in a phenomenology of perception. Rather the body is in some sense the very subject of perception.

Like Sartre, Merleau-Ponty was keen to provide a phenomenology of our essential situatedness in the world, our status as the product of accreted traditions and socio-cultural practices. Unlike Sartre, he declined to provide a theory of consciousness as a void or nothingness. The transcendental aspect of this theory was anathema to a philosophy that maintained a relentless focus on our embodied status. Among other things, this approach allowed Merleau-Ponty to develop a more congenial and politically salutary theory of intersubjectivity than Sartre's conception of competing objectifying gazes.

Later in his career, the focus on the body would give way to a more abstract and metaphysically ambiguous conception of 'flesh' as lying at the heart of all phenomenological reduction. With this gesture Merleau-Ponty gave renewed significance to a term with theological overtones and also situated his work in a tradition dating back to critiques of mechanisms that drew on more holistic theories of sensibility.

Today, one often finds Merleau-Ponty's work cited in bridge-building exercises between analytic or cognitive and phenomenological approaches to philosophy of mind. His writings on art have also garnered a wide audience, and had an impact on aesthetics and art history. His 1945 essay 'Cezanne's Doubt' is a tour de force of criticism and exemplifies themes elaborated elsewhere in his philosophy. Merleau-Ponty's approach to the late impressionist drew focus to the indeterminacy that arises whenever one seeks to distinguish between what is natural and what is artifice in a representation, artistic or otherwise.

> Cézanne did not think he had to choose between feeling and thought, between order and chaos. He did not want to separate the stable things which we see and the shifting way in which they appear; he wanted to depict matter as it takes form, the birth of order through spontaneous organization.

Cezanne's doubt, as it were, stemmed from his will to make art and nature the same, to break down the putative barrier between them.

> If I am a certain project from birth, the given and the created are indistinguishable in me, and it is therefore impossible to name a single gesture which is absolutely new in regard to that way of being in the world which, from the very beginning, is myself.

As is clear, this aesthetic investigation yielded up themes that harbour political connotations. Much of Merleau-Ponty's explicit writing on politics was bound up with polemics about the USSR.

But his distrust of totalization—the notion that our perceptual field is infinitely inexhaustible and hence never complete or totalized—inspired a generation of thinkers to be discussed in a later chapter. However, in the shorter term, Merleau-Ponty's focus on the paradoxes of embodiment, the liminal status of our subjectivity between two ostensibly incompatible substances, would continue to inspire thinkers in the years immediately after his death. Concluding his investigation into Cezanne, Merleau-Ponty had observed: 'Two things are certain about freedom: that we are never determined and that we never change'.

French epistemology and philosophy of science

Worries about determinism shaped the efforts of other French thinkers moved by the introduction of phenomenology in France. These are the philosophers of the concept in Foucault's heuristic: Jean Cavaillès, Gaston Bachelard, Georges Canguilhem, and Alexandre Koyré. Initially a historian of religion, Koyré (1892–1964) was the most sibylline among these figures intellectually. Inspired by Heidegger and his existential pathos—and thereby cross-cutting the very divide Foucault sought to establish—Koyré wrote a series of articles that culminated in a path-breaking book in the history of science, *From the Closed World to the Infinite Universe* (1957). In this book, first written in English and only later translated into French, Koyré claimed that the Copernican Revolution and in particular the work of Galileo ushered in a change of worldview without precedent—literally. Koyré's point was that the 'break' achieved in the change of outlook was not prefigured, but one that reordered our very understanding of science as a historical enterprise, establishing the infinite universe as an unending field of exploration whose perfection and coherence cannot be assumed.

A top student of Brunschvicg's, Jean Cavaillès (1906–44) was, like Merleau-Ponty, moved by Husserl's Paris lectures. Also like Merleau-Ponty, he occupied a privileged place in French academia, serving as *agrégé-répétiteur* in philosophy at the École Normale Supérieure. This was the post for the instructor charged with preparing future philosophy teachers in France for the national exam, and was the position from which Louis Althusser would exercise his influence for many years.

Husserl led Merleau-Ponty to rethink embodied experience. Cavaillès thought the ontology of intentional acts in Husserl's theory might shed light on the history of mathematics. Cavaillès saw in this history the possibility for a theory of the historical development or 'becoming' of science as such, but it was one that he was never able to complete. He was executed by the Wehrmacht in 1944 for his role in the French Resistance. Cavaillès was ultimately sceptical that a theory of science could ever ground itself in a more general theory of consciousness, be it anthropological, phenomenological, or transcendental in the Kantian sense. In such a view, we can't be sure that our efforts to know the world are not really just better ways of knowing ourselves—that is, knowing how we know it rather than knowing it directly. In contrast to Vico's *verum-factum* principle—which states that we can know what we have made, hence we can know our history, including the history of science—Cavaillès took inspiration from Spinoza's notion that *verum index sui et falsi*—the true is its own sign and that of the false. In the history of mathematics, Cavaillès saw the history of a science whose truth claims were manifestly indifferent to the 'consciousnesses' in which they were beheld. He was likewise stimulated by the fact that a science that purported to utter eternal truths had a manifestly historical emergence. Central in this regard was Georg Cantor's development of transfinite mathematics in the late 19th century. For the first time in history, a mathematician was able to demonstrate the relationship between variably sized sets with an infinite number of members. No longer potential, the infinite was now actual and multiple. This was a genuine discovery in the sense that it was in no way discernible in or predictable from earlier developments except retrospectively.

Where Cavaillès focused on mathematics, Gaston Bachelard (1884–1962) concerned himself more with physics and chemistry. In a number of books, Bachelard advanced the idea that science was a kind of applied rationalism. What he meant by this was not that theory comes first, and then practice comes along to verify it. Rather, all the practices in the scientific laboratory were theoretically mediated, that is, constructed and imbued with value by the theoretical framework. And yet, given their material and worldly status, events in the lab had the capacity to force a rethinking of the theoretical framework itself. Bachelard described such a moment as an 'epistemological rupture' or an 'epistemological break', in a manner consonant with Koyré's theses. Classic examples of such a rupture include the Copernican Revolution. Closer to the 20th century was Lavoisier's discovery that what was flammable in fire was not phlogiston, but oxygen. The recalcitrance of the world to theoretical manipulation, in the lab or out, led to a reframing of knowledge—a new set of problems to investigate rather than new answers to outstanding questions. Bachelard's work would find an analogue in the American philosopher of science Thomas Kuhn's notion of the 'paradigm shift', first introduced in his classic *The Structure of Scientific Revolutions* (1963). In this vision the history of science is not linear and cumulative, but one of intermittent periods of normal science that are upended by revolutions in theoretical frameworks. Change the frame and new objects come into view.

With thinkers considering the history of mathematics, physics, and chemistry, Georges Canguilhem (1904–96) turned his attention to the history of biology. His first major study was an enquiry into the history of the reflex concept, in which he argued that the concept stemmed not from a mechanistic view of science but a vitalistic one. Canguilhem's attitude to the history of science focused on concepts and foreswore all teleology. He was interested in tracing how concepts came to be formed and then how they were often transformed when exported beyond their original zone of signification. Within this approach to the history of science lay a profound, if obscure, thinking about notions one more typically associated with political thought. For example, one typically regards the reflex as an instance of unfreedom—it's a spontaneous act that we can't will otherwise. But Canguilhem saw in the transmutations of the reflex concept glimmers of an alternative theory of freedom grounded in responsiveness to one's own environment. One way to think of Canguilhem's work is as the de-vitalizing of Bergson's vitalism. The metaphysical element of the *élan vital* was out of play by the middle of the 20th century. But Canguilhem nonetheless saw value in Bergson's theory of life as a theory of environmental mediation and a striving towards homeostasis. The essays in his collection *Knowledge of Life* (1952) play up the notion that knowledge does not confront life from without, but is part of life. Practical knowledge is always oriented in one way or another, and at root theoretical knowledge is itself a kind of practical knowledge insofar as it sustains or negates life. Here too we see Nietzsche's influence on Canguilhem's work.

His major study, *The Normal and the Pathological*, was defended as a thesis in 1943, like Sartre's and Merleau-Ponty's studies, during wartime. His history of the genesis of these concepts and their parasitic relationship on one another would be absolutely crucial for Michel Foucault and his early enquiries into the history of madness.

As with the existentialists, we must remember the political context of Canguilhem's own writing. Cavaillès enlisted him in the Resistance and he served as a medic for wounded fighters. Canguilhem would later devote a book to Cavaillès's memory in which he could not but contrast Cavaillès's active engagement with the more esoteric variety undertaken by Sartre. The action-oriented elements of the French epistemologists of this era would later inspire structuralists such as the Marxist Louis Althusser and his students in their rebuffs to the speculative elements of existentialism. The resonance between political activity and philosophical content can be over-stated. Yet the

French sociologist, Pierre Bourdieu, once observed that there did seem to be a class character distinguishing existentialism and epistemology in the period that explained the former's tendency towards totalization and the latter's preference for fragmentation. Sartre descended from the Parisian *haute-bourgeoisie*. Cavaillès and Canguilhem hailed from the provinces; and Bachelard was a postman before turning to philosophy later in his life.

The critiques of totalization that one finds emergent in Merleau-Ponty's work and throughout the epistemologists laid the ground for some of the most difficult and nevertheless provocative writings of 20th-century philosophy—writings variously grouped as structuralist or post-structuralist. As wartime passions cooled and political energies turned towards de-colonization and the fate of Communism, philosophy moved away from an existentialist focus on the subject towards approaches to political, social, and scientific problems that challenged the humanism Sartre embraced as a slogan for his doctrine. These philosophical developments also involved an openness to other modes of thought, such as psychoanalysis and anthropology. The structuralist moment of the 1960s will occupy us in Chapter 6.

Chapter 6
Restless times: structuralism and post-structuralism

Recent scholarship has done much to change our understanding of the philosophical efforts that first came to be recognized under the name 'French Theory'. Through a series of transmissions in the 1960s, 1970s, and 1980s, readers in North America, the UK, and Australia were introduced to the names Foucault and Derrida, among many others. Often associated with 'postmodernism'—a term that first emerged in architecture—this body of work coalesced around a number of themes: a critique of the 'philosophies of the subject' that had persisted through existentialism; an anti-humanism that seemed to verge on nihilism; a scepticism of progressive philosophies of history that culminated in Jean-François Lyotard's diagnosis of 'the postmodern condition' as one defined by incredulity towards master narratives, be they of a liberal or a Communist character. Much of this writing was also marked by a literary bent. Among the factors that made it 'theory' rather than philosophy in a traditional sense were a persistent reference to the arts and a style that often demanded something more like aesthetic interpretation than engagement at the level of argument.

Our historical understanding of the theory boom in the humanities is a work in progress and truly a transnational story, distinct in certain respects from philosophical developments internal to France. For example, it is often remarked that the

French themselves rarely distinguished between structuralism and post-structuralism. But the fact is there was a shift in the tenor and content of French philosophy between the 1960s and the 1970s, one that the staggered timing of translations overseas tended to obscure. Here one event or, rather, a pluralized set of 'events' stands out among others: the array of political acts and consequences gathered in the name 'May '68'.

The student and worker revolts of this moment put a halt to the scholastic quality that had been the hallmark of mid-1960s structuralism. Instead, thinkers began to talk about desire and affect with an emphasis on their collective dimensions. Works like Deleuze and Guattari's *Anti-Oedipus* (1972) and Lyotard's *Libidinal Economy* (1974) further pursued the philosophical integration of Marxian and Freudian perspectives that had been under way since the interwar years. But they did so in a manner that stressed indeterminacy and spontaneity and often took the form of a rejection of the systematizing tendencies found in historical materialism and psychoanalysis.

The 1970s also saw the advent of *écriture feminine*, or 'women's writing'. Associated with the names Luce Irigaray (1930–), Hélène Cixous (1937–), Catherine Clément (1939–), and Julia Kristeva (1941–), this experimental mode of thought drew on ideas to be discussed in this chapter in order to develop a feminism that refused the categories that still informed Simone de Beauvoir's approach. Rigorous in its aesthetic formalism but difficult to parse in terms of its theoretical content, *écriture feminine* remains one of the major legacies of French post-structuralism.

But if the distinction between structuralism and post-structuralism belongs primarily to a reception history, what relevance does it have for French philosophy per se? Here the main development took place in 1966, in the famous conference at Johns Hopkins University devoted to 'The Language of Criticism and the Sciences of Man'. The event was designed to take stock of the structuralist turn away from existentialism in French thought. Special emphasis was placed on Claude Lévi-Strauss's anthropology, although the psychoanalyst Jacques Lacan was also present and notoriously left the conference organizers with a hefty phone bill after haranguing Lévi-Strauss and others in Paris throughout the night with reports on the American scene. The key moment of the affair was Jacques Derrida's lecture 'Structure, Sign, and Play in the Discourse of the Human Sciences'. Scholars had gathered to gain a better sense of a mode of thought that prioritized the relational rather than the representational elements of a discourse, scientific or otherwise, and drew its authority from the writings of the Swiss linguist Ferdinand de Saussure (1857–1913). Lévi-Strauss had repurposed a theorization of language that suspended any putative reference to the world in order to make sense of culture as a code the anthropologist might decipher. Derrida's lecture suggested that any effort to establish such a discourse, such a code, could not but make clear an element of play and instability at the very heart of language itself. A 'discourse' is constitutively unable to determine where it ends and its outside begins. 'Post-structuralism' was born from the sense that efforts to identify specific discursive structures were no less doomed to failure than earlier efforts to limn the features of phenomenological consciousness.

The convergence of effect between two disparate events—a 1966 conference in Baltimore and a nationwide political upheaval in France two years later—in the explanation of shifts in French philosophy is fitting, given that a major theme of the philosophy in this era concerned the contingent nature of historical change. But equally important is the continuity this period bears with earlier developments. Structuralism and post-structuralism are both marked by a heavy use of neologism, one that is inviting or irritating depending on one's taste. But the penchant for linguistic invention is itself significant insofar as it is indicative of a philosophical effort that is haunted by its history, yet striving to produce something new. As noted, among the general themes of the moment was a hostility to progressive philosophies of history, which was often encapsulated in a general antipathy towards Hegelianism. But as Michel Foucault cannily remarked, Hegel had made negation part of his system; perhaps his greatest ruse lay in the fact that every effort to escape his influence left you face-to-face with him.

This significance accorded to a 19th-century German idealist calls for explanation. In a recent reflection on the 1960s in French thought, the philosopher and linguist Jean-Claude Milner remarked that his generation came to university with a sense that German could no longer be the language of philosophy because of the Nazi catastrophe and that English 'had long since ceded to market forms'. This made French philosophy the inheritor of a history and a vocation. Yet he also remarked that, with the benefit of hindsight, he thought this sense of grandiosity, 'these games around language', amounted to a mirage.

Our task then is to account for the innovation and energy of this moment, but also its illusions. The focus will be on three thinkers each in different ways emblematic of the period: Michel Foucault, Jacques Derrida, and Gilles Deleuze. But before we consider these thinkers whose works spanned the era, a better sense of the discrete features of the structuralist moment itself is in order. It is now clear that phenomenology was not so much eclipsed by structuralism as mediated by it. But it is equally clear that the structuralist moment in 1960s philosophy was characterized by a greater openness to discourses that historically had not only been outside of philosophy but hostile to it: psychoanalysis and historical materialism. To be sure, existentialists also engaged with Freud and Marx. But for the structuralists, the paradoxical virtue of these transgressive 'human sciences' lay in their exposure of philosophy's limitations.

Structuralism between Freud and Marx

Beyond Lévi-Strauss, the two major figures identified with 'high structuralism' were Lacan and the Marxist philosopher Louis Althusser. Lacan's rethinking of Freud began in the interwar years. He too was present at Kojève's lectures. Over the course of a controversial career, one that saw his expulsion from the International Psychoanalytic Association, Jacques Lacan (1901–81) did his utmost to eliminate from the Freudian project any traces of biological determinism and its normative focus on adaptation as a goal of psychoanalytic practice. Focusing on language, Lacan eventually developed a recondite schema of the real, the imaginary, and the symbolic, that reproduced (or replaced) Freud's tripartite presentation of id, ego, and superego. For Lacan, the realm of conscious experience, the 'ego', was an imaginary domain in the sense that it served as a mediating screen that at once presented and obscured the reality of our subjectivity (a 'real' in which one might locate the 'id') and the moral authority of the symbolic order of language, a repurposed notion of the superego. Lacan's teaching is impossible to summarize—not least because it was always undergoing revision. But the signal innovation of his project was not simply to rename Freud's categories but to rethink their relation to one another.

In Lacan's vision, the real and the symbolic are intimately related, to a point of near indeterminacy between them. This is because we are not simply buoyed by language from the outset of our lives but in effect we are constituted by it. Lacan notoriously said 'the unconscious is structured like a language'. We emerge into consciousness via a play of signifiers and our subjectivity is located in the interstices. Note that, notwithstanding the structural tenor of his approach, Lacan's project carried forth a reworking of Cartesian themes that were present in Sartre and Merleau-Ponty. Far from being hostile to Cartesianism, Lacan saw in it something like the birth of modernity—the moment when subjectivity was first recognized as a kind of vanishing point, a condition of all representation that itself could never be represented.

Sartre became increasingly Marxist over the years, culminating in his second mammoth work *Critique of Dialectical Reason* (1960). Regrettably for Sartre, the project was more or less dead on arrival and here the main reason lay in the energy gathered around a philosophy professor at the École Normale Supérieure who also happened to be a member of the French Communist Party, Louis Althusser (1918–90). From his position as *agrégé-répetiteur*, Althusser inspired a generation of students in the early 1960s who were keen to rediscover a Marxism shorn of the humanist tendencies found in French existentialism. Through a series of articles that were eventually published as *For Marx* (1965) and a collective seminar with his students published as *Reading Capital* (1965), Althusser insisted that the science of historical materialism implicit in *Capital* was achieved by an 'epistemological break' with the humanism of Marx's early writings. Borrowing heavily from the French epistemological tradition, Althusser developed an interpretation of Marx that was as intellectually galvanizing as it was philologically dubious. His major provocation was to suggest that the turn to humanism in Marxist thought in the wake of Khrushchev's 1956 secret speech addressing Soviet crimes was not an antidote to Stalinism but an exacerbation of it. In Althusser's optic, humanism and Stalinism both participated in the broadly Hegelian error of thinking that history had a progressive tendency that might be made legible and then implemented politically. In contrast, the theory of history developed in *Capital* was one of discrepancies between levels of society; political change was a matter of contingency, the seizure of a moment created by the 'over-determination' (a term borrowed from psychoanalysis) of weak points in a set of political relationships. The exemplum of such a situation for Althusser was Russia in 1917.

It's important to appreciate the irony of Althusser's celebrity in the 1960s. Here was a philosopher who rejuvenated Marxism by convincing its newest adherents that Communism was in no sense guaranteed and that one could not act under the conviction that history proceeded in any discernible order. Yet he married these heterodox ideas to an overwhelmingly rationalist account of Marxism as a science that would always be able to account for history's retrospective intelligibility. Althusser cited Comte as a forebear in this regard, and many in Western Marxism were quick to discern a positivism in Althusser's thought all the more distressing for its apparent hostility to experimental refutation. The philosophical task was to generate a 'theory of theoretical practice' through which Marxism would be able to understand the role of all discourses—ideological or scientific—in the maintenance of exploitative social relations. Such would be a necessary prelude to any potential transformation of them.

The intersection of the Lacanian and Althusserian projects reached an apogee in the *Cahiers pour l'Analyse* (1966–9), a journal run by young *normaliens* that used resources from these two 'masters' as well as French epistemology and analytic philosophy to articulate a general theory of structure and subjectivity at the most abstract level possible. Its final issues were in press once the May events got under way and most of its authors disappeared into the Maoist radicalism of the Gauche Proléterienne and other far left groups in the 1970s. Among these thinkers was Alain Badiou, who would acquire a much greater audience in France, and overseas, in the 21st century.

Protestors in 1968 proclaimed that structures don't take to the streets. Lacan saw the spontaneity of the events as evidence that they in fact do—the structure in question being that of adolescent revolt and the quest for a master. So in some sense May '68 was both the consummation of structuralism and its dissolution. But to consider the three major philosophers whose work straddles this event is to see the myriad ways history can have—or not have—an effect on philosophy. For Michel Foucault, May '68 gave a new political inflection to his work, one that would dominate it through the 1970s. For Jacques Derrida, May '68 seems more like a non-event, its effects hardly legible in the development of deconstruction and its increasingly international context. Finally, for Gilles Deleuze, May '68 was the catalyst that took him from writing heterodox works of history of philosophy and metaphysics to producing some of the most emblematic works of 1970s radicalism with his collaborator Félix Guattari.

Foucault

Born in Poitiers in 1924, Michel Foucault entered the École Normale Supérieure in 1946. He was an isolated student who quickly came in contact with Althusser and developed an early filiation with Marxism. His main influence in the period however was Georges Canguilhem, who inspired Foucault to focus on the history of science. Yet throughout his studies of psychology and the history of medicine in the 1950s, Foucault remained engaged with the literary avant-garde situated around such figures as Maurice Blanchot, and he also developed a strong acquaintance with German thought, above all Friedrich Nietzsche and Martin Heidegger.

Foucault has always been difficult to classify in a disciplinary sense—he was as much a historian as a philosopher. Yet despite the typically voluminous source base he deployed in his studies, the real force of his work came from the overarching theoretical unity they comprised. This comes out in his first major study, his primary thesis, completed in 1960 and devoted to 'the history of madness in the classical age'. Its title in French—*Folie et déraison (Madness and Unreasonableness)*—pointed to the relationship between the terms, treating the former not as the absence of reason, but as something that bore a necessary relationship to it as a kind of 'unreason'. Foucault was interested in a historical transformation whereby the 'mad' went from being considered part of society to an element excluded from it in its very constitution. In a provocative reading, Foucault suggested Descartes' *Meditations* were emblematic of this shift. In his attempt to ground the authority of reason, Descartes first had to flirt with madness, to feign madness as someone who doubted the reality of his surroundings. Reason's reign was established once the mad were excluded from its domain. Not coincidentally, a young Derrida would target this aspect of Foucault's reading, suggesting that the mechanics of exclusion were not so clear-cut.

The *History of Madness* established Foucault's reputation and other works on the history of medicine followed. His most 'structuralist' book was *The Birth of the Clinic* (1963), which gave an account of how pathologies were constructed and apportioned under the objectifying gaze of medical practice. This book developed further Foucault's insights regarding the relationship between truth and power. As doctors came to discover the truth of bodies, they further inscribed subjects in regulatory systems of understanding that at once enabled and constrained their actions.

In 1966, Foucault published *The Order of Things* (in French: *Les mots et les choses*), a book that expanded the method deployed in the early works and served as well as 'an archaeology of the human sciences'. Foucault pursued three related shifts in our understanding from the classical to the modern age: from natural history to biology, from grammar to linguistics, and from a science of wealth to economics. All three movements participated in a general shift towards considering 'man' the object of knowledge. Foucault was concerned to show that the modes of thought in the two periods—his term of art to describe the governing norms of understanding in an epoch was 'episteme'—were incommensurable, and here we see the affiliation with French epistemology and hear echoes as well of Kuhn's notion of the 'paradigm shift'. More to the point, he sought to uncover the peculiar feature of this object of study in the modern age. The figure of man was, in Foucault's understanding, an 'empirico-transcendental doublet'. Trading on ambiguities in Kant's philosophy—Kant was an emblem of this shift as Descartes had been before—Foucault noted that 'man' was at once the authority of knowledge, its transcendental ground, and also the very object of investigation, its empirical concern. This resulted in a situation in which knowledge generated its own obscure points. For example, biology as the science of life never figures forth life as such; it is strictly speaking unrepresentable in itself. Life is the object of study but also the condition of possibility for the science that is to discover it. The criteria of understanding are shown to be historically mutable.

This historical element is crucial. And *The Order of Things* infamously concludes with a passage that suggests as much. Foucault writes:

> One thing in any case is certain: man is neither the oldest nor the most constant problem that has been posed for human knowledge. Taking a relatively short chronological sample within a restricted geographical area—European culture since the sixteenth century—one can be certain that man is a recent invention within it. It is not around him and his secrets that knowledge prowled for so long in the darkness. In fact, among all the mutations that have affected the knowledge of things and their order, the knowledge of identities, differences, characters, equivalences, words—in short, in the midst of all the episodes of that profound history of the Same—only one, that which began a century and a half ago and is now perhaps drawing to a close, has made it possible for the figure of man to appear. And that appearance was not the liberation of an old anxiety, the transition into luminous consciousness of an age-old concern, the entry into objectivity of something that had long remained trapped within beliefs and philosophies: it was the effect of a change in the fundamental arrangements of knowledge. As the archaeology of our thought easily shows, man is an invention of recent date. And one perhaps nearing its end.

If those arrangements were to disappear as they appeared, if some event of which we can at the moment do no more than sense the possibility—without knowing either what its form will be or what it promises—were to cause them to crumble, as the ground of Classical thought did, at the end of the eighteenth century, then one can certainly wager that man would be erased, like a face drawn in sand at the edge of the sea.

Hence Foucault's 'anti-humanism'. Foucault's powerful diagnosis made *The Order of Things* a bestseller in Paris, no doubt more discussed than read. But it was read with much interest by the editors of the *Cahiers pour l'Analyse*, who put to Foucault a series of questions that would lead him to produce the initial draft of *The Archaeology of Knowledge* (1969). This difficult text sought to defend Foucault's brand of discourse analysis, but its framework was quickly left behind.

The *Cahiers'* editors had asked Foucault who his real authority was: Freud or Nietzsche. No serious reader could think Foucault would prefer the former. Subsequent years would see work deeply inspired by Nietzsche's thought, in particular his genealogical conception of historical change as a story driven by mutations in power arrangements. In the wake of 1968, Foucault briefly ran the experimental philosophy department at Vincennes. But an appointment at the Collège de France in 1970 put him back in the centre of French academic life.

His first several years of lecture courses at the Collège culminated in *Discipline and Punish: The Birth of the Prison* (1975). Inspired by his work with activist groups on behalf of prisoners, Foucault produced a study that again traced major changes between the early modern and late modern periods. Whereas before punishment had been a matter of spectacle, now it was shunted away from society. Whereas before discipline had been a matter of bodies in their exposure, now it became a matter of internal regulation. Inverting Christian themes, Foucault suggested 'the soul is the prison of the body'. His reading of Jeremy Bentham's panopticon project—a prison arrangement in which prisoners could surmise they were being surveilled without knowing for sure—was an evocative metaphor for our situation in the modern age. We are surrounded by signs and injunctions—all so many governmental techniques in which we actively participate—that show that power is not centralized, but something that exists in a network of relations.

As ever, Foucault quickly subjected his published work to revision. Future courses at the Collège would explore themes of sovereignty and governmentality, providing alternative histories of liberalism along the way. Much of this work was developed into Foucault's ambitious *History of Sexuality* project. The first volume, *The Will to Know* (1976), appeared shortly after *Discipline and Punish*. Here the provocation was to challenge a history of sexuality as a history of repression, and to suggest instead that the very notion that there was an aspect of our being that was exclusively 'sexual' and capable of being 'repressed' was itself an instance of specifically modern, regulatory ways of thinking.

This initial volume still bore the traces of Foucault's discursive and epistemic focus. His later lectures and writings would witness a turn to the ancients to uncover the deepest sources of our ways of thinking about the self as an object of care and concern and the practice of truth-telling as central to the formation of subjectivity in all its forms across the ages.

Foucault's accomplishment was overwhelming by any standard. And there is virtually no area of the humanities or social sciences that has been untouched by his effort. While visiting Berkeley in the early 1980s, he produced a short text that revisited Kant's answer to the question 'What is Enlightenment?' Always concerned to produce a properly historical understanding, Foucault contrasted, not his answer, but his very question to Kant's:

> But if the Kantian question was that of knowing what limits knowledge has to renounce transgressing, it seems to me that the critical question today has to be turned back into a positive one: in what is given to us as universal, necessary, obligatory, what place is occupied by whatever is singular, contingent, and the product of arbitrary constraints? The point in brief is to transform the critique conducted in the form of a necessary limitation into a practical critique that takes the form of a possible transgression.

Foucault's approach to this question was equally ethical and political, which shows that his nominal 'anti-humanism', far from being a species of nihilism, was part of a more general legacy of the Enlightenment, thereby linking Foucault's project with a longstanding set of philosophical commitments in France. Others of the moment were more sceptical.

Derrida

Jacques Derrida (1930–2004) has been among the most celebrated French philosophers overseas, but also among the most derided. When Cambridge University proposed to credit his achievements with an honorary degree in 1992, many on the philosophy faculty voiced their opposition to celebrating such a 'charlatan'.

What made Derrida's work such a neuralgic point for philosophers? The answers are several and speak to the nature of his accomplishment, which was characterized by a corrosiveness towards rationalism and systematic thought the likes of which hadn't been seen since the rediscovery of Pyrrhonism in the early modern period. And indeed Derrida is perhaps best regarded as descending from a Montaignian moment in French philosophy, which we can contrast with the Cartesian one.

We've mentioned the event that made his name internationally, his critique of Lévi-Strauss at the Johns Hopkins conference in 1966. The focus on discourse in this lecture did much to shape Derrida's initial reception as a thinker concerned above all with language. Other writings of the 1960s, such the essays in *Writing and Difference* (1967) and *Of Grammatology* (1967), added to this emphasis.

At the heart of Derrida's engagement with structuralism lay a scepticism towards the notion that writing is best conceived as derivative of language's more basic form: the spoken word. Through readings of Plato and others, Derrida aimed to show that any attempt to privilege speech over writing was based on a fundamental instability. At the root of meaning-making, Derrida argued, was a primary form of inscription grounded in our nature as temporal beings. To write is to leave a trace, to inscribe. It is an externalization of meaning that is itself a condition of possibility for any future meaning-making. Consider that all speech participates in a code that is prior to it. We do not create the language we speak. Derrida's contention that 'there is nothing outside the text' (*il n'y a pas de 'hors-texte'*) can be understood in a manner analogous to Bishop Berkeley's idealist principle *esse est percipi*, which we can paraphrase as that there is nothing outside perception. Any gesture outside of the text—the set of marks, in whatever form, that makes intelligibility possible—carries the text forward. We don't get outside meaning-making.

And in fact to make meaning always requires remaking it. For a sign—be it a word, mark, or signature—to be intelligible, it must be endowed with 'iterability', that is, the capacity to be repeated elsewhere and retain its meaning. But this very feature of meaning, as it were, also means that meaning is always subject to erasure, given that we can't control which aspects of meaning will carry over and which won't. The sense of our utterances is never fixed and stabilized.

Derrida expanded on these ideas in his critique of Lévi-Strauss's reliance on Rousseau to make sense of the effects of the 'writing lesson' on the Nambikwara peoples in South America. Any attempt to privilege an original 'nature' that is prior to 'culture', and yet has the potential to be corrupted by it, already presupposes forms of meaning-making that are prior to the positing of that originary nature. Karl Kraus, the Austrian critic and inspiration for many German intellectuals, had said 'origin is the goal'. Derrida showed that the origin is elusive. Here we see that not only is meaning always subject to potential erasure. In its lack of fixity, it is also always deferred, an idea Derrida expressed with the term *différance*—a quasi-portmanteau that captures the senses of difference and deferral in a new noun.

Derrida's strategy is clear. He purports to make manifest ostensive binaries—speech and writing; nature and culture; the normative and the descriptive—and to reveal the indeterminacy between them. Any attempt to establish the integrity of a concept calls upon a supplement on which it is parasitic and from which it distinguishes itself. This method—although Derrida insisted that it wasn't a method to be applied but an 'event' that was always, already at work—was termed 'deconstruction'.

At its best, deconstruction can reveal mechanisms of exclusion, rhetorical or otherwise. At its worst, deconstruction becomes less a vehicle of understanding than conjecture. If there is nothing outside the text, and if meaning is never stable, how could one's understanding of a text be contested one way or another? Lévi-Strauss suggested Derrida handled the law of the excluded middle in his work 'with all the delicacy of a bear'. That Lévi-Strauss failed to recognize himself in Derrida's description hardly counted as an objection, for the context of his utterances, to say nothing of his intentions, was no constraint on Derrida's understanding. A deconstructionist can always challenge an appeal to context by pointing to the instability between the text and its context. In this, deconstruction was a radical hermeneutic that often treated texts more as occasions for philosophical rumination than objects of interpretation. This galvanized literary scholarship, but many were troubled when deconstructive strategies moved beyond the aesthetic domain to law, politics, and indeed philosophy.

In the scandal of this approach and its breadth of application lay Derrida's historical significance. For deconstruction was not so much a new kind of reading as a deepening and further development of Heidegger's thought in the French context. Heidegger described his project in 'fundamental ontology' as the *Destruktion* of the history of metaphysics. Derrida claimed to go one stage further by chasing out the 'metaphysics of presence' that informed *all* philosophy, up to and including the 'onto-theology' of Heidegger's own thought. In Derrida's view, the history of modern thought was motivated by the desire to preserve presence—expressed in a number of surrogate concepts, for example substance, essence, *ousia*—over absence. All our modes of representation, from language to art to science, were captive to this logic, which Derrida regarded as violent. But deconstruction could show presence always slipping away, always intercalated with the very absence it tries to exclude.

We are now far from structuralist linguistics. If he was initially associated with structuralism, Derrida's project is increasingly understood in terms of its place in the history of French phenomenology. Many of his earliest writings were on Husserl. His Master's thesis, written in 1953–4, dealt with 'the problem of genesis in Husserl's phenomenology' and he translated Husserl's late writing 'The Origin of Geometry' and published it with an extended introduction in 1962. When considered in light of another of his writings of the period, *Voice and Phenomenon* (1967), on Husserl's theory of signification, it becomes clear that Derrida's work belongs in—and complicates—the bifurcated reception history of phenomenology noted in Foucault's schematic.

For it's equally clear that Derrida privileges neither 'consciousness' nor the 'concept' in his work. The very opposition is of course ripe for deconstruction. But Derrida's engagement with Husserl was itself mediated through theological elements present in Husserl's initial French reception, such as the writings of Christian existentialists like Gabriel Marcel. The ground sought in Husserl's phenomenological reduction always proved to be no ground at all, only present in its absence, only knowable in its being beyond knowledge. Derrida's thinking on religion is mercurial and not unrelated to the features of his own biography. Born in Algeria to a Jewish family, Derrida never professed any adherence to the faith, but the sense of marginality that accompanied his arrival in Paris to pursue his studies left its mark. Derrida's writing on Jewish themes, often in conjunction with his assessments of other Jewish thinkers such as Walter Benjamin, are among his most illuminating, which makes the Christian element of his engagement with Husserl all the more provocative.

A final note on politics. Unlike Foucault, for whom politics was never far from his concerns, especially after 1968, Derrida was for many years reticent on political questions, leading to charges of nihilism. Part of this derived from an aversion to any philosophical vindication of political views that stemmed from his years teaching alongside Althusser at the École Normale Supérieure in the 1960s. (Derrida was quite fond of Althusser personally; his grievances were more with the Althusserians.) But in later years, Derrida increasingly turned his attention to questions of justice. In Derrida's understanding, justice could never be the result of a calculation, much as forgiveness couldn't be the product of a reasoned or instrumental decision. If the outcome is determined, rationally or, worse, algorithmically, in what sense is the outcome 'just'? It simply is. Acts of justice—be they via tribunals of restitution or reconciliation—are always haunted by their indeterminacy and the notion that injustice might prove ineradicable. The world will not provide the answer, nor will it validate it. Despite Derrida's distance from Sartre, it's hard not to see the persistence here of existentialist themes.

Deleuze

The 1970s saw Foucault turning more to history and politics and Derrida expanding his deconstruction of philosophy with writings on Hegel and Nietzsche. Others were inspired to a new thinking about affect and desire that bore untimely affinities with an earlier, vitalist moment in French philosophy.

Deleuze and Guattari and Lyotard were leading figures, but this is also the moment when *écriture féminine* truly got under way. For philosophy to link up with history, it needed to link up with the corporeal domain, dealing with bodies rather than signifiers, attending to the micropolitics of desire. The collaboration between Gilles Deleuze (1925–95) and Félix Guattari (1930–92) is exemplary of this development. The two works they published under the collective title *Capitalism and Schizophrenia*, *Anti-Oedipus* (1972) and *A Thousand Plateaus* (1980), were genre-bending exercises, allegorical and conceptual in equal measure. Talking of fluxes and flows and smooth versus striated spaces, Deleuze and Guattari had a vision of history as driven by 'desiring-machines' (akin to Sartre's 'being-for-itself' or Heidegger's *Dasein*—yet another sobriquet for the human) that were impervious to negation. Foucault called *Anti-Oedipus* a manual for non-fascist living. Against a Hegelian philosophy of history, driven by the labour of the negative, Deleuze and Guattari promoted a vision of pure production and positivity. It's important to hear in 'positivity' not just an evaluative position, but an echo of positivism. What you see you is what get; yet the world is infinite and inexhaustible in the data it yields up to inform our practices.

Deleuze's collaboration with the renegade psychoanalyst Guattari would have been hard to predict in the previous decade. The initial stages of Deleuze's career were devoted to works in the history of philosophy, with volumes on Hume, Kant, Nietzsche, Bergson, and Spinoza. These culminated in his doctoral thesis *Difference and Repetition* (1968), a dense work of philosophy that recast metaphysics in the terms of its title. Taken together, these terms suggest something analogous to Derrida's notion of iterability. But Deleuze's focus was hardly linguistic, dealing instead with an unusual range of writings on time, representation, and mathematics. Some references were recognizable, for example Kierkegaard. Others weren't. It's hard to imagine another philosopher of the moment citing Jozef Maria Hoene-Wronski's 1819 treatise on the philosophy of the infinite. In the conclusion to *Difference and Repetition*, Deleuze forwarded a quintessentially non-modern view as an alternative to post-Heideggerian efforts to think the relation between the temporal and the conceptual: the scholastic thesis associated with Duns Scotus regarding 'the univocity of being'. To say being is 'univocal' is to say that it speaks with one voice, 'a single and same Ocean for all the drops'. It is to indicate that there is no hierarchy within creation, and especially no hierarchical distinction between concept and affect, thought and body. Given the metaphysical attack on hierarchy his work comprised, perhaps Deleuze's later collaboration with anarchist political tendencies is no surprise at all.

Deleuze occupies a peculiar place in recent French philosophy, on the one hand as a thinker associated with radical political movements, and on the other as a philosopher devoted to producing works that, in their unbridled metaphysical aspirations, seemed out of step with deconstructive scepticism. In later years, Deleuze would resume writing in his own name, with difficult books on cinema written in a Bergsonian key; and an ingenious interpretation of Leibniz as a 'baroque' philosopher. He also wrote a short, illuminating book on Foucault. The two would fall out over their attitude to 'The New Philosophers', a group of young, anti-totalitarian intellectuals who took over the airwaves in the late 1970s. Deleuze saw them offering liberal bromides to an exhausted culture; Foucault shared their anti-Marxism enough to endorse them for a spell.

Deleuze's final work before his death was another collaboration with Guattari: *What is Philosophy?* (1994). Among other things, this book saw the culmination of a pragmatist tendency in Deleuze's thought, one present in his writings on Bergson and American literature. Philosophy was defined as the creation of concepts, and therefore as a practical activity. But as a practice it was also grounded in affective schemes. The question to ask a concept is, what does it do? What does it *produce*, affectively or otherwise? Deleuze saw this orientation as consistent with Spinozism, which he deemed a 'practical philosophy', given that its author purported to see in his difficult rationalist constructions not an abstract philosophy, but rather a 'meditation on life'.

Deleuze's Bergsonism and Spinozism are evidence of the historically conditioned character of French philosophy, even of the most radical and innovative sort. It is not the least of the ironies of this moment that a philosophical effort devoted to thinking about the creation of the new—and lauded overseas, particularly in the Anglophone world, for its novelty—should be so steeped in tradition. Chapter 7 will take stock of the consequences of this moment, with emphasis on the legacies of deconstructionism and Althusserianism. But it will also consider two of the most salient features of contemporary French philosophy: the new forms of political philosophy that emerged in the 1980s and the theological turn in phenomenology.

Chapter 7
French philosophy today: competing ambitions

In 2004 Alain Badiou penned an essay on a moment in French philosophy for which he took himself to be the latest, and most likely the last, representative. Stretching from the end of the Second World War to the end of the century, this period bore comparison with classical Greece and the concentrated output of German Idealism at the cusp of the 19th century. No doubt self-serving, Badiou's approach is nevertheless suggestive for the way it positions philosophy as an activity that is at once universal in its aspiration and yet always specific in the forms it takes. One need not agree with Badiou that philosophy is perforce universal in order to find his description of a cultural moment that regarded itself in such terms as apt.

More apt still is the way in which the claim to specificity seems to be a ruse. 'All contemporary French philosophy is also, in reality, a discussion of the German heritage,' he writes. But he also points to the distinction between 'concept' and 'life' as central to French philosophy since Brunschvicg and Bergson. We've already seen Foucault's heuristic for making sense of phenomenology's reception in France get displaced ever farther into the past. Why not then go back to Parmenidean 'being' in its opposition to Heraclitean 'flux' to frame philosophy's essentially dialectical nature? The reference to the ancient Greek and modern German contexts in Badiou's essay is a means to vindicate the vocation of French philosophy.

This ambitious self-understanding is what distinguishes French philosophy from its Anglophone and German counterparts today. Be it the critical theory of Jürgen Habermas or the conservatism of students of Reinhart Koselleck, German philosophy operates in a manner distrustful of the grandiose. The modus operandi of analytic philosophy, prevalent in the Anglophone world, is there in the name. In this vision, the task of philosophy is to break problems down into smaller, tractable parts. To be sure, there has recently been an uptick of metaphysics in an analytic mode. But its style has none of the historical gravitas of the French approach.

If French philosophy remains unified by speculative daring, in other ways it is fragmented. The best we can do in this concluding chapter is to provide a survey of current tendencies in the field. As ever, a guiding theme is the way in which innovation itself seems to be grounded in a historical orientation. The first two sections will consider the legacies of Althusserian Marxism and Derridean deconstruction. The final two consider the development of a new approach to political philosophy that emerged in tandem with movements of historical revisionism in the 1970s, and the 'theological turn' that has taken place in French phenomenology.

After Althusser

'Althu sert à rien'—Althusser is worthless. Such read the graffiti in May 1968. The effects of this revolt led to the diminution of his stature over the course of the 1970s. The end of his influence came in 1980, when, in a psychotic episode, Althusser strangled his wife to death. Granted a non-lieu by the state due to his medically diagnosed dementia, Althusser avoided criminal proceedings and spent the remainder of his days in palliative care. He died in 1990.

Add to this the declining fortunes of Marxism in the 1980s and the explosion of post-structuralist scepticism in the academy, and a significant Althusserian legacy seems unthinkable. No doubt many of his students have had productive careers.

Pierre Macherey is one of Spinoza's leading interpreters in France and has been for decades. Étienne Balibar, perhaps Althusser's closest confidant, has made a name for himself with trenchant writings on liberal themes. But only recently has the importance of the Althusserian moment for making sense of contemporary philosophy in France become clear.

Crucial in this development have been the contributions of two philosophers who emerged from the Althusserian milieu: Jacques Rancière and Alain Badiou. These thinkers are among France's most visible today and they each have carved out unique personalities and projects. Even so, we can trace the roots of their work to a reckoning with the consequences of Althusser's intervention in French Marxism.

Though he purports to have been an Althusserian for only about five minutes, Jacques Rancière (1940–) was a contributor in the 1960s to the *Capital* seminar and resulting publication. His 1975 tract *Althusser's Lesson* distilled a generation's hostility to their mentor's disdain for spontaneous revolt. Contained in this polemic was a categorical rejection of philosophy and its claims to authority in the field of politics. Rancière spent much of the 1970s writing for *Revoltes Logiques*, a heterodox historical journal that was not far from Foucault's work of the period. The idea was less to fit historical actors into Marxist frameworks and more to let them speak for themselves.

This aspect of Rancière's approach reached its apogee in his doctoral thesis, *Proletarian Nights: The Worker's Dream in Nineteenth Century France* (1981). Breaking with the decorum of professional historiography, Rancière wrote in the free indirect style of Flaubert a work that integrated citation and paraphrase. The texts in question were those produced by artisans and workers in the hours away from the shop. Here was a theme Rancière would develop in subsequent work. Equality is less a principle than a fact affirmed by subjects in their actions. If a proletarian's place is in the factory, the penning of poetry during time designated for rest refuses this 'place'.

The impetus of the book was anarchic, and liberalism and Marxism were equally in Rancière's sights, as they were in the minor thesis that accompanied this study, entitled *The Philosopher and his Poor* (1983). Here Rancière explored references to the 'poor' in the philosophical canon from Plato onwards. The final chapter delivered a leftist critique of the esteemed French sociologist, Pierre Bourdieu, a leftist himself. In his investigations of the uses of cultural capital to perpetuate forms of discrimination in educational institutions, Bourdieu under-valued the capacity of students to make their own meaning, to refuse the place given to them. An extreme expression of Rancière's contrasting pedagogical vision can be found in his short book, *The Ignorant Schoolmaster* (1987), devoted to the 19th-century pedagogue, Joseph Jacotot. Jacotot's claim to fame was his ability to 'teach' a classroom of students who spoke Flemish even though he did not. In this practice, Rancière saw 'the equality of intelligences' at work.

In the past two decades, Rancière has become best known for his writings on aesthetics, which emerged from his reflections on history-writing and political philosophy. Challenging canons of modernism, Rancière finds in the arts not a site of elite distinction, but a space in which ways of seeing are constantly reframed and new forms of experience are brought into being by spectators and practitioners alike. Many late 20th-century philosophers found in Kant's aesthetics new ways for thinking about politics in an age of unrepresentable catastrophe. For Rancière, nothing is off limits to representation. 'The distribution of the sensible' in his vernacular (*'le partage du sensible'*) is always being transformed by spectators who see and act in different ways.

Rancière's work seems far afield from Althusser's today, but in its hostility to teleological conceptions of history we see lingering effects of this early teaching. But this influence—if that's what it is—is largely offset by Rancière's hostility to rationalist philosophy. In this, too, he can be contrasted with the most notorious post-Althusserian of the age, from whom we've already heard: Alain Badiou (1937-).

Though never a student of Althusser's, Badiou made contributions to the *Cahiers pour l'Analyse* in the 1960s that marked him out as one of the most vociferous proponents of Althusserian 'science', a disposition all the more striking given that until that point Badiou had been attempting fiction in a Sartrean mode. After years of Maoist radicalism following May '68, Badiou produced a staggering treatise that unified the Sartrean and Althusserian elements of his formation. *Being and Event* (1988) began with the bold claim that 'mathematics is ontology', meaning that whatever can be said of being *qua* being is said by mathematics. The use of Cantorian set theory to argue for the ontological priority of inconsistent multiplicity over unity was heterodox at a minimum. Recourse to ancient Greek paradoxes and their modern mathematical avatars were for Badiou an entrée into a work of philosophy that challenged the Heideggerian privilege accorded to finitude that, in his view, had dominated French philosophy since the Second World War.

With his title, Badiou inscribed his project in a 20th-century lineage. Much as the 'nothingness' of subjectivity was opposed to the 'being' of objectivity in Sartre's philosophy, Badiou used 'event' to name that which is not expressed by ontology. Given that being 'in itself' is nothing but inconsistent multiplicity for the atheist Badiou, the question becomes how anything becomes consistent at all. How are there 'subjects' who perform 'actions' that have meaning and coherence? For Badiou, the subject emerges in the wake of a rupture in the order of things. More, the subject is that individual who recognizes that an 'event' has taken place and reordered 'being' where others might not.

The political radicalism of Badiou's vision is clear. A revolutionary is precisely one who believes a revolution has taken place. But Badiou saw this phenomenon at work in scientific and artistic innovation as well. The figure of the unrecognized genius who comes to be understood only through tenacious fidelity to his discoveries is a frequent one in Badiou's writings.

Perhaps most significantly, a key model for the militant subjectivity that Badiou promoted in his work came from yet another context. In a book entitled *Saint Paul: The Foundation of Universalism* (1998), Badiou made a virtue of the fact that the truth to which Paul bore witness was one that was not demonstrable but instead predicated on faith. Badiou's own failure to believe Paul, that is, to be a Christian, did nothing to mitigate Paul's status as an exemplary figure able to forge a collective endeavour on the strength of his fidelity to an event deemed truly to have taken place. In one of the earliest critical engagements with his thought, Slavoj Žižek observed that Badiou's theory of the subject, in this and other instances, was essentially the same as Althusser's, albeit with the valuation reversed. For Althusser, subjects are produced by an ideology which 'hails' them in the same way a police officer hails a suspect on the street. One becomes a subject when one recognizes oneself in the call, a process Althusser called 'interpellation'. Likewise, Badiou's subjects depend on the events to which they bear witness. But instead of being bridled by ideology, Badiou's subjects become vectors of the truths—artistic, scientific, political—they have discovered.

Since *Being and Event*, Badiou has produced two other major works fleshing out his philosophical system and deepening his engagement with mathematics, *Logics of Worlds* (2006) and *The Immanence of Truths* (2018). These works have also sought at length to introduce more robust criteria for discerning events, and for distinguishing subjects faithful to truths from a contrast class of 'obscure' or 'reactive' subjects who, while cognisant of events, are so in such a way that mitigates or negates the truths they generate—with catastrophic results. Badiou's achievement is monumental, in a dual sense—as both an imposing accomplishment, but also as something of a memorial. Recognition of this feature increasingly seems to be part of Badiou's self-understanding, as can be seen in his reflections on a waning moment of French philosophy and in his abiding predilection for modernist figures and the 20th century more generally.

Destinies of deconstruction

In its ability to account for so many phenomena in terms of the unique ontological framework on offer, Badiou's system, devoted to newness, can nevertheless create a sense of closure. It is a philosophy to which one subscribes rather than a set of claims about which one might be persuaded. Deconstruction was largely developed against the hermeticism of Althusserian science, which persists in Badiou's project, but it too risked descending into an incantatory practice. If deconstruction is always already at work in every discourse, what innovation could it harbour?

A number of former students of Derrida have developed his thought in new directions, though it is an open question whether they have moved past the orbit in which Derrida's own thought moved. Jean-Luc Nancy (1940–) for years collaborated with Philippe Lacoue-Labarthe on explorations of romanticism that made manifest Derridean and Heideggerian themes in that movement. In later work, Nancy began to write in a more political key. With books like *The Inoperative Community* (1983) and *Being Singular Plural* (1986), Nancy explored the ways in which the form of being-with—what Heidegger called *Mitsein*, a notion also crucial to Simone de Beauvoir—was an essential feature of political life. But in this ontologically primordial 'being-with', Nancy saw an impossible project, a constant breaking down of communication and thwarted collectivity. Whatever the grounds, the community is something that cannot be disclosed to, or discovered within, the community itself. More, the quest for such grounds is often what renders a community inoperative.

Nancy has recently undertaken an ambitious deconstruction of Christianity that is being pursued in dialogue with thinkers identified with the theological turn in phenomenology. For Nancy, Christianity is the supreme case of a deconstruction that is always already at work in history, and indeed our contemporary moment ought to be regarded in such terms. In this, Nancy is close to others, such as Charles Taylor, who have argued that the secular age is best understood in its historical and metaphysical relationship to the era out of which it emerged.

Derrida has long been associated with a certain anti-scientism, a charge which is largely unjust given how much his early work looked at cybernetic and biological sciences. But it is nevertheless surprising that two of the most prominent developments in deconstruction have taken a scientific turn. Bernard Stiegler and Catherine Malabou have each pushed the limits of deconstruction by focusing on technology and the neurosciences, respectively.

Bernard Stiegler (1952–) discovered Derrida's work while serving time in prison for petty theft. It's a remarkable origin story, one that Stiegler has himself written about in a philosophical key. Moved by Husserl's writings on time in a space where the passing of time was distended, Stiegler took up a correspondence with Derrida that developed into a mentor–mentee relationship.

Stiegler's first major work, his doctoral thesis, was entitled *Technics and Time*. Subtitled *The Fault of Epimetheus*, in reference to the ancient Greek god who lacked his brother Prometheus's foresight to give to humans any traits to distinguish them from other animals, it was also identified as 'volume 1', a sign of the prodigiousness to come. In an analysis that relied as much on the anthropologist André Leroi-Gourhan as Heidegger's

Being and Time, Stiegler proceeded to argue that the human being is well and truly the product of technology and not the other way around. Deploying Derridean themes, Stiegler understands 'technics' as a process of the exteriorization of memory. Tools are those ways in which animals build an environment. But that environment in turn conditions all that can be accomplished within it. The trace logic that Derrida deemed central to deconstruction is here at work. Each tool leaves a mark on the world; but every technical innovation can equally be forgotten. In Stiegler's speculative anthropology, the technical epigenesis of the human essentially *has* been forgotten, which is why we are all endowed with the 'fault' or 'lack' that comes from Epimetheus's original forgetting. The human being becomes nothing more than the exhaustive potential of technological development.

Stiegler developed the *Technics and Time* project in two further volumes. Other multi-volume works bearing the titles *Disbelief and Discredit* and *Symbolic Misery* have explored the ways in which contemporary techno-capitalism has impoverished our capacity as meaning-making animals. In some sense, Stiegler's writings have a conservative quality. It's not for nothing that one of his political writings is entitled *The Re-enchantment of the World* and seeks to mobilize notions of 'spiritual value' against 'industrial populism'. Victor Cousin may have said the same thing in the 19th century, minus the deconstructive armature.

A different approach to science can be found in the work of Catherine Malabou (1959–), who was one of Derrida's collaborators towards the end of his life. At the centre of Malabou's work is the concept of 'plasticity', drawn from her investigations into the neurosciences. Plasticity describes the dual capacity to bestow and receive form, as in the 'plastic arts'. But it can also apply to that which destroys form, as in plastic explosives. It is paradoxical in that it contains notions of durability, mutability, and finality in a single concept. And in all these ways the brain is essentially plastic.

Malabou has explored plasticity in a variety of venues, in works on Hegel and Heidegger, but also in an engagement with psychoanalysis entitled *The New Wounded* (2007). Arguing against a conception of subjectivity oriented around sexuality, Malabou proposed a concept of 'cerebrality' to talk about the brain as the very site of subjectivity and its possible transformations. This move alone is enough to distinguish her from a tradition of thought that was largely hostile to thinking about the mind or subjectivity in anything like physiological terms. Yet, for Malabou, brain damage is an instance of a kind of trauma that cannot be captured, much less healed or reversed, with the symbolic resources of psychoanalysis or philosophy. If this seems obvious, the innovation of Malabou's work is to see the material forms described by neurology precisely as forms amenable to deconstruction. Their enabling and constraining properties cannot be prised from one another. This irreducibly material element of our being and sense of self and its capacity for radical transformation lies at the heart of what Malabou elsewhere calls the 'ontology of the accident'.

Malabou's focus on the contingent has put her in dialogue with another contemporary philosopher, Quentin Meillassoux (1967–), a student of Badiou's. But where Meillassoux seeks to ground a new rationalism based on 'the necessity of contingency', in effect aiming to overturn the Kantian resolution to Hume's challenge to metaphysics, Malabou regards her work as essentially post-deconstructive. In other words, rationalism is not a live option. Rather, philosophy needs to honour what was best in deconstruction by tracing the materiality and ephemerality of forms as they are disclosed to us by the contemporary sciences.

Political philosophy—'the Revolution is over'

The politics of post-Althusserianism and deconstruction are to be found at a recondite level. In this, it stands in contrast to a style of political philosophy that also emerged out of postwar Marxism but that has come to take on a distinctly historical form. The most visible contemporary representatives of this approach are Marcel Gauchet and Pierre Rosanvallon. But each can trace his investigations of the vicissitudes of French republicanism to the example set by Claude Lefort (1924–2010) and his collaborations with the Greek expatriate Cornelius Castoriadis (1922–97).

Members of the French Communist Party at the end of the Second World War, Lefort and Castoriadis represented the Trotskyist wing and moved quickly away from any officially sanctioned form of Marxism with the establishment of the movement and journal *Socialisme ou Barbarie* in 1948. Convinced that Stalinism would continue without Stalin, Lefort took to investigations of the history of political thought under the guidance of Maurice Merleau-Ponty. Lefort's doctoral study on Machiavelli was an ambitious, Proustian volume that investigated how political stability was always a work in progress given the absence of any transcendent authority. Themes from his mentor infused the work—a scepticism of totalizing visions, and a phenomenological attentiveness to political experience as forged in the encounter between mutually regarding (and often hostile) subjects.

These ideas found an echo in Lefort's collaborations with Castoriadis, which also drew upon Lacan's theorization of fractured subjectivity in ways that departed from the Althusserians' structural approach. Lefort's later writings on sovereignty in the modern age increasingly circled around the notion that democracy is grounded on a void that cannot be represented or occupied. Totalitarianism emerges from a tendency inherent in democracy itself to occlude this void, to claim a kind of transhistorical legitimacy for a political programme. Really existing Communism was in the background to Lefort's concerns, but it also received vindication in historiographical developments of the 1970s.

In 1978, the historian François Furet published a book entitled *Penser la Révolution française* (*Interpreting the French*

Revolution) that began with the pronouncement: 'the Revolution is over'. Furet's point was that two centuries of debate over the meaning of the Revolution was enough, and that a renewed investigation of the history of the event showed that it was not to be explained by the socio-economic factors common to Marxist and conservative interpretations, but instead as an instance of politics in its symbolic capacities 'skidding out of control'. In effect, Furet provided a Lefortian interpretation of the Revolution itself. The Terror resulted from a kind of foreclosure of the space left vacant by the displacement of the king. Democracy as contestation was intolerable and unstable. Revolt against oppressive political structures would always have the tendency to produce new forms of violence in turn. But absent any divinity, the authority would become something like 'history' itself with political actors claiming to have divined its tendencies. But it is such claims to history's meaning or direction that tend to vouchsafe political catastrophe. The Cold War context of this writing is evident.

The convergence of Lefort's political philosophy with Furet's approach to history led in the 1980s to new forms of long-term historical thought that broke with Marxism and the anti-historicism of deconstruction. In 1984, Marcel Gauchet (1946–) published *The Disenchantment of the World: A Political History of Religion*. Trading on Max Weber's diagnosis of modernity, Gauchet reversed the terms of a Marxist approach that sees religion as the epiphenomenal expression of social conflict in order to argue that our very conception of society is itself the consequence of the rendering immanent to this world of a divine authority heretofore deemed transcendent to it. Borrowing from Foucault and Lacan as well, Gauchet in this work laid the foundations for a counter-history of modernity that resulted in the four-volume study *L'Avènement de la democratie* (*The Advent of Democracy*, 2007–17). Here Gauchet traced the manner in which democracy came to be regarded as the only viable source of political legitimacy, not because of its foundations in a theory of rights, but precisely due to the absence of any foundations at all.

A contest in its essence, Gauchet's democracy is like Plato's *pharmakon* in Derrida's reading, both poison and cure.

Gauchet's influence was disseminated via the journal he founded in the 1980s, *Le Débat*, and the Fondation Saint-Simon, which had been founded by Furet and Pierre Rosanvallon (1948–). Like Gauchet, Rosanvallon has come to be known for ambitious historical writings infused with philosophical sensibility. After early works that sought to recover under-appreciated thinkers in the history of French republicanism, for example Guizot and Tocqueville, Rosanvallon turned his sights to the history of democracy in France. His titles suggest the themes and the connections with Lefort's legacy: *Le Peuple introuvable* (*The Missing People* 1998), *La Democratie inachevée* (*Incomplete Democracy* 2000), *La Sacre du citoyen* (*The Sacred Citizen* 2001). Themes of fracture and incompleteness link this work to that produced in a deconstructive or post-Althusserian key. But the historical substance of these studies is what distinguishes them; their speculative register is offset by an appeal to the historical record.

Arguably the most distinguishing feature of Gauchet's and Rosanvallon's work, however, is to have brought the question of religion back to the centre of politics. The deep irony in Furet's pronouncement that 'the Revolution is over' is that the nature of the debate over political legitimacy absent religious authority seems as vibrant and crisis-ridden as ever. It also points to the persistence of Christian themes in French philosophy from the early modern period into the present day. Nowhere is this more evident than in the contemporary status of phenomenology in France.

A theological turn?

In 1991, Dominique Janicaud published a short, polemical text entitled *The Theological Turn in French Phenomenology*. Though phenomenology was secular or at any rate agnostic in its original formulation, Janicaud's worry was that phenomenology in France had turned its sights to those phenomena that were precisely not discernible by the senses. If Jean Wahl had urged his compatriots to turn 'toward the concrete', as his 1932 book had it, phenomenology had taken a turn away from the world to precisely those areas one would have thought beyond the domain of phenomenological description. How did this happen?

In Janicaud's telling, Merleau-Ponty was the French philosopher truest to phenomenology's agenda. With his late focus on the arts, he never lost sight of the sensible element essential to the enterprise. In contrast, Merleau-Ponty's contemporary Emmanuel Levinas (1906–90) had moved phenomenology in a different direction with his major studies, *Totality and Infinity* (1961) and *Otherwise than Being* (1974). Arguing against Heidegger, these books posited that the ethical relation to 'the Other' was prior to all others—even to our self-relation as temporal beings. But essential to Levinas's view was the notion that 'the Other' could never be an object of representation; the other is in that sense 'beyond being'. We can phenomenologically investigate this relationship, but what we find is that one pole of the relationship seems to occupy a space that cannot be known positively. Steeped in Jewish learning, Levinas brought themes from the Talmud to bear in his phenomenological investigations and seemed to open the door to dialogue between phenomenology and negative theology. One of Derrida's earliest writings concerned the 'violence' he saw as still too present in Levinas's approach to metaphysics. But Levinas no doubt played a more positive role in Derrida's own later explorations of religion.

Besides Levinas, another figure implicated in the theological turn was Paul Ricoeur (1913–2005), a noted interpreter of Freud, among other things. Yet whatever religious elements were in Ricoeur's project, they were by and large muted, or at any rate kept distinct from his phenomenological approach. His writings on time, narrative, history, and memory required no reader to share his Protestant commitments for them to be illuminating.

In this, Ricoeur was to be contrasted with Michel Henry (1922–2002), in whose 'phenomenology of life' Janicaud saw a betrayal of phenomenology in the service of theology all the more dismaying for being surreptitious.

Henry's first major work, *The Essence of Manifestation*, appeared in 1963. A gargantuan study, even by French standards, Henry argued that the phenomenological tradition, from Husserl through to Heidegger, Sartre, and Scheler, remained captive to what Henry termed 'ontological monism'. What Henry meant by this was that, even though someone like Heidegger insisted on an 'ontological difference' between being as a verb and beings as existents, in the end being only knew one form of appearing, that of transcendence, that is, the fact of appearing outside our consciousness in time. We tend to think of transcendence as otherworldly; for Henry, transcendence is precisely the defining feature of this world, the world of appearance, because everything that appears to us, appears to transcend us in its very appearance.

Indeed, Henry traded on the phenomenological (and perhaps common sense) point that everything that appears to us appears outside of us and in time. But what Henry argued over hundreds of pages was that this kind of being—the being of appearing—only exists because of a more primordial kind of being that doesn't appear at all, the being of 'life' as 'auto-affection'. Life, in Henry's understanding, is totally immanent to itself and never comes outside itself. Biological or physiological efforts to describe life mistake it in its essence, for they make it a datum among others in the world; they make 'transcendent' what is truly 'immanent'. But for Henry life is precisely that which is not in the world, because it is the fact of the world's appearing at all. In this sense, life is 'the essence of manifestation'.

The theological themes of Henry's approach are suggestive and they were clear in subsequent works that considered Marx in such terms and a 'genealogy of psychoanalysis' that revealed life's occluded status. In his final years, Henry's writings dealt explicitly with theology. In *I Am the Truth: Toward a Philosophy of Christianity* (1996), Henry read the Christian tradition as speaking to the 'truth of life' as opposed to the 'truth of the world'. In writings from the same period, Henry made clear that with the collapse of structuralism and other fashions in the human sciences, 'phenomenology seems increasingly to be the movement of the thought of our times. The "return of Husserl" is the return of the capacity for intelligibility.'

Henry thought phenomenology and theology were distinct but complementary enterprises. Their distinction has been repeatedly defended by the last figure dealt with in Janicaud's account, who is also one of France's most esteemed living philosophers: Jean-Luc Marion (1946–). Marion first made his name with a series of studies devoted to Descartes and a work that has come to be central to postmodern theology entitled *God without Being* (1981). Invoking themes that go back at least to Thomas Aquinas, Marion argued that, given that no predicate is adequate to God, not even being itself, God is essentially without being. The fact of existence—of being itself—cannot be explained by an appeal to being.

Beyond Descartes' scholarship and theology, the third element of Marion's career has been phenomenology. In a series of works which show their debt to Henry, Marion has argued that, after Husserl and Heidegger, a third phenomenological reduction is required. Husserl reduced phenomena to their dependence on intentional consciousness, and Heidegger went further by reducing them to the consequences of our finitude. Marion says a third reduction treats the phenomenon as a matter of pure givenness. Once we bracket out all of the sensible particularities of a phenomenon what remains is the fact of that phenomenon's being given at all. Marion has used this approach to illuminate all manner of quotidian activities and arts. But his ultimate purpose is to use the phenomenology of givenness to make sense of what he calls 'saturated phenomena'. These are those phenomena that are so overflowing, so in excess of any conceptual capture, that they cannot be represented at all. Certain works of art or the experience of love might fit this description. But the *locus classicus* of the saturated phenomenon for Marion is that of revelation.

There's nothing surreptitious about Marion's Catholicism. He was an adviser to Pope Benedict XVI and is explicit about his religious commitments. Janicaud's worries about a theological turn in French phenomenology are evocative of worries that have attended modern French philosophy for centuries in its apparent inability to have done with a religious heritage. But there is also plenty of work being done by French phenomenologists, for example Renaud Barbaras (1955–) and Claude Romano (1967–) that, while in dialogue with the tendency represented by Marion, is hardly exhausted by a religious orientation. Indeed, Romano's work has striven to put phenomenology in conversation with kindred developments in analytic philosophy concerned with meaning and representation, such as the writings of Donald Davidson and John McDowell. Henry's approbation of phenomenology has the flavour of an apology in the theological sense, sure to aggravate those who see phenomenology as now captive to a theological agenda. But his notion that it seems to be 'the movement of thought of our times' does express something of its status in contemporary France, where phenomenology seems to be the most forward-looking and proliferating research programme.

There is irony in this, given that so much 20th-century French philosophy was a reckoning with the impact of phenomenology, and that many of the most ambitious philosophical projects—from Althusser's Marxism to Derrida's deconstruction—were themselves efforts to articulate alternatives to the horizon provided by Husserl and Heidegger. But the historical orientation remains strong, perhaps definitive, in French philosophy.

And if the modern age seems to be defined by a series of conflicts—between objectivity and subjectivity; reason and affect; science and religion—then French philosophy seems destined to remain a site of battle between tendencies which, if history is any guide, appear to depend on one another.

Chapter 8
Conclusion

In a 1958 essay devoted to the history of psychology as a discipline, Georges Canguilhem noted that when one exits the Sorbonne on the rue Saint Jacques, one has two options. Go up the hill and you arrive at the Panthéon; opt for the other direction and you find yourself heading toward the Préfecture de Police. The metaphor was not particularly subtle, even if it was still illuminating. The human sciences in France had the potential for greatness. But they could also easily be instruments of state power and control.

The Panthéon towers over the Latin Quarter, where most of Paris's educational institutions are located. Conceived as a church, the structure was completed more or less just as the French Revolution got under way. It was quickly recast as a secular mausoleum intended to honour great French people. Over the course of Paris's tumultuous history, it has periodically reverted to its religious function, but today it stands as a monument to France's intellectual and political greatness. Inside, one can find Foucault's Pendulum, proving that the Earth turns on its axis. If one descends into the crypt, one finds buried a number of statesmen alongside the scientists Pierre and Marie Curie, the novelists Victor Hugo and Émile Zola, and the great Enlightenment *philosophe*, the Marquis de Condorcet. Most prominently displayed are the tombs of Voltaire and Jean-Jacques Rousseau.

Next to the Panthéon is Saint-Étienne du Mont, a Gothic church that dates from the 15th century, although the site itself has served as that of a chapel since the 6th century. The church contains the shrine of Sainte Geneviève, the patron saint of Paris, who was to be honoured by the structure of the Panthéon in its original conception. To this day the devout make pilgrimages to the Mont Sainte Geneviève—the hill on which both the church and the Panthéon are located—to honour her memory. This building also contains tombs. In addition to the remains of Paris's patron saint, there are those of Jean Racine, the great dramatist of the 17th century, and Blaise Pascal, the physician, mathematician, Catholic theologian, and philosopher from the same epoch.

The Panthéon positively dwarfs Saint-Étienne du Mont. Crowding it out of the Place du Panthéon itself, it appears to be pushing it down the hill toward the Seine. But the fact is that the church is still there, obdurate. And even if Voltaire's and Rousseau's tombs are boldly displayed for the glory of secular France, Pascal's remains, marked by an inconspicuous epitaph, are not far away.

This instance of urban planning tells us something about French philosophy, historically and presently. Centuries of innovation have sought to displace the authority of the Church in matters scientific, political, and philosophical. But the displacement has yet to be complete. Students at the leading high schools of Paris make their way past both the Panthéon and Saint-Étienne du Mont as they prepare for their exams. Like students across the country, they are required to take a capstone course in philosophy in order to receive their degrees.

In 1990, Pierre Macherey wrote an essay in which he sought to define 'la philosophie à la française'. Setting aside the commonality of language and cultural markers—such as those one might use to distinguish French cuisine—he concluded in ways evocative of Canguilhem's concerns several decades before. French philosophy is and has been characterized above all by the way the French put philosophy into practice, which is by and large via institutions that bear some relationship to the nation-state. This can be seen in the centrality of philosophy to education. But it's also discernible in the wide array of state-sponsored grants and organizations that fund philosophical research in France to this day. And given that the history of the French state is one that has been driven by contestation and fundamental questions about the possibility of establishing non-religious foundations of legitimacy, it stands to reason that French philosophy would be marked by similar traits—and this notwithstanding the omission of Saint-Étienne du Mont from Canguilhem's cartography.

References

Works listed in this section are primary sources either cited directly or discussed at some length in the main chapters. Where it exists, an English translation has been cited. Secondary sources are listed in the Further reading section.

Chapter 2: The origins of French philosophy

P. Charron, *A Treatise on Wisdom* (London: Forgotten Books, 2017).

R. Descartes, *The Philosophical Writings* (3 vols, Cambridge: Cambridge University Press, 1985–91).

R. Descartes, *The World and other Writings* (Cambridge: Cambridge University Press, 1998).

N. Malebranche, *The Search after Truth* (Cambridge: Cambridge University Press, 1997).

M. de Montaigne, *The Complete Essays* (London: Penguin, 2004).

Chapter 3: Radical philosophy: the 18th century

J. D'Alembert, *Preliminary Discourse to the Encyclopedia of Diderot* (Chicago: University of Chicago Press, 1995).

E. Condillac, *Essay on the Origin of Human Knowledge* (Cambridge: Cambridge University Press, 2001).

D. Diderot, *Rameau's Nephew/D'Alembert's Dream* (London: Penguin, 1976).

J. Locke, *An Essay Concerning Human Understanding* (Oxford: Oxford University Press, 1979).

J.-J. Rousseau, *The Basic Political Writings* (Indianapolis: Hackett, 2012).

Chapter 4: Post-Revolutionary philosophy: the 19th century and the Third Republic

H. Bergson, *Matter and Memory* (Cambridge, MA: Zone Books, 1990).

L. Brunschvicg, *Les Étapes de la philosophie mathématique* (Paris: Blanchard, 1981).

A. Comte, *The Positive Philosophy of August Comte* (3 vols, Cambridge: Cambridge University Press, 2009).

N. de Condorcet, *Political Writings* (Cambridge: Cambridge University Press, 2012).

J. Lively, ed., *The Works of Joseph de Maistre* (New York: MacMillan, 1965).

F. Ravaisson, *Of Habit* (London: Continuum, 2008).

Chapter 5: Philosophy in wartime: phenomenology and existentialism

S. de Beauvoir, *The Second Sex* (New York: Vintage, 2011).

J. Cavaillès, *On Logic and the Theory of Science* (Falmouth and New York: Urbanomic/Sequence Press, 2020).

M. Foucault, 'Life: Experience and Science', in James D. Faubion, ed., *Aesthetics, Method, and Epistemology* (New York: The New Press, 1998).

E. Husserl, *Cartesian Meditations* (Dordrecht: Kluwer, 1999).

A. Kojève, *Introduction to the Reading of Hegel* (Ithaca, NY: Cornell University Press, 1980).

M. Merleau-Ponty, 'Cezanne's Doubt', in Thomas Baldwin, ed., *Merleau-Ponty: Basic Writings* (London: Routledge, 2003).

M. Merleau-Ponty, *Phenomenology of Perception* (London: Routledge, 2013).

J.-P. Sartre, *Being and Nothingness* (London: Routledge, 2018).

J.-P. Sartre, *Nausea* (New York: New Directions, 2013).

Chapter 6: Restless times: structuralism and post-structuralism

L. Althusser, *For Marx* (London: Verso 2005).

G. Deleuze, *Difference and Repetition* (New York: Columbia University Press, 1994).

G. Deleuze and Félix Guattari, *Anti-Oedipus: Capitalism and Schizophrenia* (Minneapolis: University of Minnesota Press, 1983).

J. Derrida, *Writing and Difference* (Chicago: University of Chicago Press, 1980).

J. Derrida, *Of Grammatology* (Baltimore, MD: Johns Hopkins University Press, 1974).

M. Foucault, *The Order of Things* (New York: Vintage, 1994).

L. Irigaray, *Speculum of the Other Woman* (Ithaca, NY: Cornell University Press, 1985).

J. Lacan, *Ecrits* (New York: Norton, 2006).

P. Rabinow, ed., *The Foucault Reader* (New York: Pantheon Books, 1984).

Chapter 7: French philosophy today: competing ambitions

A. Badiou, *Being and Event* (London: Continuum, 2005).

A. Badiou, *The Adventure of French Philosophy* (London: Verso, 2012).

A. Badiou, *Saint Paul: The Foundation of Universalism* (Stanford, CA: Stanford University Press, 2003).

M. Gauchet, *The Disenchantment of the World: A Political History of Religion* (Princeton: Princeton University Press, 1999).

M. Henry, *The Essence of Manifestation* (Dordrecht: Kluwer, 1973).

M. Henry, *I am the Truth: Toward a Philosophy of Christianity* (Stanford, CA: Stanford University Press, 2002).

M. Henry, *Material Phenomenology* (New York: Fordham University Press, 2008).

D. Janicaud et al., *Phenomenology and the Theological Turn: The French Debate* (New York: Fordham University Press, 2001).

C. Lefort, *Machiavelli in the Making* (Evanston, IL: Northwestern University Press, 2012).

C. Malabou, *The Future of Hegel: Plasticity, Temporality, and Dialectic* (London: Routledge, 2004).

C. Malabou, *The New Wounded: From Neurosis to Brain Damage* (New York: Fordham University Press, 2012).

C. Malabou *What Should We Do with Our Brain?* (New York: Fordham University Press, 2008).

J-L. Marion, *Being Given: Toward a Phenomenology of Givenness* (Stanford, CA: Stanford University Press, 2002).

J-L. Marion, *God without Being* (Chicago: University of Chicago Press, 2012).

Q. Meillassoux, *After Finitude: An Essay on the Necessity of Contingency* (London: Continuum, 2010).

J. Rancière, *Aisthesis: Scenes from the Aesthetic Regime of Art* (London: Verso, 2013).

J. Rancière, *Proletarian Nights: The Workers' Dream in Nineteenth-Century France* (London: Verso, 2012).

J. Rancière, *The Philosopher and his Poor* (Durham, NC: Duke University Press, 2004).

C. Romano, *At the Heart of Reason* (Evanston, IL: Northwestern University Press, 2015).

P. Rosanvallon, *The Demands of Liberty: Civil Society in France since the Revolution* (Cambridge, MA: Harvard University Press, 2007).

B. Stiegler, *Technics and Time, I: The Fault of Epimetheus* (Stanford, CA: Stanford University Press 1998).

Further reading

French writing on French philosophy is beyond voluminous and in many instances the line between commentary and contribution is unclear. This selection focuses on English-language secondary literature on French philosophy, although some works in translation are listed.

General works

D. Clarke, *French Philosophy, 1572–1675* (Oxford: Oxford University Press, 2016). A thorough, very readable account from one of the most eminent scholars of early modern French philosophy.

V. Descombes, *Modern French Philosophy* (Cambridge: Cambridge University Press, 1980). Cambridge commissioned this book from a practitioner of French philosophy and the result was published in English prior to a French edition that appeared under the title *Le Même et l'autre* (*The Same and the Other*). It remains useful for seeing the ways in which French philosophy developed under the shadow of German influence.

G. Gutting, *French Philosophy in the Twentieth-Century* (Cambridge: Cambridge University Press, 2001). A helpful survey that is especially good in its introductory chapters, which cover 19th-century thinkers rarely discussed in Anglophone scholarship.

J. Jennings and M. Moriarty, eds., *The Cambridge History of French Thought* (Cambridge University Press, 2019). A collection of commissioned articles that situate French philosophers among other developments in modern French thought. State of the art.

L. Kritzman, *The Columbia History of Twentieth-Century French Thought* (New York: Columbia University Press, 2007). A vital reference work, this book has sections arranged by theme, by movement, and by individual thinker.

Chapter 2:   The origins of French philosophy

S. Gaukroger, *Descartes: An Intellectual Biography* (Oxford: Oxford University Press, 1998). An intellectual biography of Descartes that puts his work in the context of his interests and those of his contemporaries, by contrast with the more usual 'father of philosophy' approach.

S. Gaukroger, J. Schuster, and J. Sutton, eds., *Descartes' Natural Philosophy* (London: Routledge, 2000). The most comprehensive collection of articles on Descartes.

L. Joy, *Gassendi the Atomist* (Cambridge: Cambridge University Press, 1997). An excellent account of the philosophy of an unaccountably neglected philosopher.

M. Screech, *Montaigne and Melancholy* (London: Penguin, 1991). One of the most important treatments of Montaigne, which does not simply focus on his 'scepticism', as do many accounts.

Chapter 3:   Radical philosophy: the 18th century

S. Gaukroger, *The Collapse of Mechanism and the Rise of Sensibility* (Oxford: Oxford University Press, 2010). Philosophical coverage of the *Encyclopedia* and French 18th-century thought more generally.

J. Riskin, *Science in the Age of Sensibility* (Chicago: University of Chicago Press, 2002). Fascinating account of French 'sentimental empiricism'.

P.H. Reill, *Vitalizing Nature In the Enlightenment* (Berkeley: University of California Press, 2005). An excellent account of Enlightenment thinking about natural processes.

Chapter 4:   Post-Revolutionary philosophy: the 19th century and the Third Republic

C. Armenteros, *The French Idea of History: Joseph de Maistre and his Heirs, 1794–1854* (Ithaca, NY: Cornell University Press, 2011). A deeply-researched volume written by a partisan to many of

Maistre's views. Useful mainly for situating his work in a longer tradition of French philosophical thinking about history.

Maine de Biran, *The Relationship between the Physical and the Moral in Man*, ed. Darian Meacham and Joseph Spadola (London: Bloomsbury, 2016). Though it reproduces Maine de Biran's text, the volume is most helpful for the secondary chapters situating his work in the 19th century.

S. Guerlac, *Thinking in Time: An Introduction to Henri Bergson* (Ithaca, NY: Cornell University Press, 2006). A work that seeks new recruits for Bergson's perspective today and provides a chronological overview of his writing along the way.

S. Luft and Fabien Capeillières, 'Neo-Kantianism in Germany and France', in Keith Ansell Pearson and Alan D. Schrift, eds., *The History of Continental Philosophy*, vol. 3 (Chicago: University of Chicago Press, 2010). Crucial resource for approaching Brunschvicg, who awaits book-length treatment in English.

M. Pickering, *Auguste Comte* (3 vols, Cambridge: Cambridge University Press, 1993–2009). The definitive account of the life and works of Comte.

Chapter 5: Philosophy in wartime: phenomenology and existentialism

S. Geroulanos, *An Atheism that is Not Humanist Emerges in French Thought* (Stanford, CA: Stanford University Press, 2010). This book locates the common ground of existentialism and post-structuralism in theological debates and arguments about philosophy of science in the interwar years. Especially good on Kojève, a very difficult thinker to place.

E. Kleinberg, *Generation Existential: Heidegger's Philosophy in France, 1927–1961* (Ithaca, NY: Cornell University Press, 2005). A reliable account of the initial wave of Heidegger's reception in France.

D. Lecourt, *Marxism and Epistemology: Bachelard, Canguilhem and Foucault* (London: New Left Books, 1975). This study by a student of Althusser's remains helpful despite its author's having a dog in the fight as to the virtues of the French epistemological tradition for Marxism. Though inroads have been made, French epistemology and philosophy of science is a historical subject ripe for further research.

S. Moyn, *Origins of the Other: Emmanuel Levinas between Revelation and Ethics* (Ithaca, NY: Cornell University Press, 2005). Similar to

Kleinberg's volume, this study clarifies much about the initial reception of Husserl and Heidegger in France, in addition to providing an illuminating assessment of the theological element in Levinas's thought.

K. Peden, *Spinoza Contra Phenomenology: French Rationalism from Cavaillès to Deleuze* (Stanford, CA: Stanford University Press, 2014). Though arguably too captive to Foucault's heuristic, this book contains much discussion of the reception of phenomenology among philosophers of science and historians of philosophy hostile to existentialism in the years surrounding the Second World War.

H. Spiegelberg, *The Phenomenological Movement* (Dordrecht: Kluwer, 1994). Classic, comprehensive account, whose chapters on France remain essential reading.

Chapter 6: Restless times: structuralism and post-structuralism

E. Baring, *The Young Derrida and French Philosophy, 1945–1968* (Cambridge: Cambridge University Press, 2014). A contextualist study that also pays close attention to Derrida's philosophical engagement with Husserlian phenomenology and Christian existentialism, this work illuminates deconstruction and a forgotten decade in French philosophy—the 1950's—in equal measure.

J. Bourg, *From Revolution to Ethics: May '68 and Contemporary French Thought* (Montreal: McGill-Queens University Press, 2007). A vibrant account of the ethical turn in the wake of May '68, which shows the ways in which the event's radicalism was channelled into institutional forms. Especially good at situating Deleuze and Guattari's project in a wider context.

F. Cusset, *French Theory: How Foucault, Derrida, Deleuze, & Co. Transformed the Intellectual Life of the United States* (Minneapolis: University of Minnesota Press, 2008). Journalistic in tone and borderline jocose, this volume nevertheless sheds light on a moment in cultural history that continues to play out in debates about the humanities academy today.

P. Deutscher, *A Politics of Impossible Difference: The Later Work of Luce Irigaray* (Ithaca, NY: Cornell University Press, 1992). A lucid introduction to the work of a major figure in French feminism who moved beyond psychoanalysis and deconstruction in creative ways.

H. Dreyfus and Paul Rabinow, *Michel Foucault: Beyond Structuralism and Hermeneutics* (Chicago: University of Chicago Press, 1983). Classic account of Foucault's project to which Foucault himself contributed. Still repays reading for making sense of the development of Foucault's method.

S. Geroulanos, *Transparency in Postwar France: A Critical History of the Present* (Stanford, CA: Stanford University Press, 2017). A sequel of sorts to the author's previous book, listed above, this self-described 'semiotic history' delivers a vast portrait of postwar French philosophy unified around the critique of transparency as a value to be promoted.

M. Hägglund, *Radical Atheism: Derrida and the Time of Life* (Stanford, CA: Stanford University Press, 2008). A controversial volume that sets its sights on theological interpretations of Derrida's thought, this book presents deconstruction as a project grounded in a conception of radical finitude that deepens and expands Heidegger's project in exclusively atheistic directions.

P. Hallward and Knox Peden, *Concept and Form*, vol. 1: *Key Texts from the* Cahiers pour l'Analyse, and *Concept and Form*; vol. 2: *Essays and Interviews on the* Cahiers pour l'Analyse (London: Verso, 2012). This two-volume set reproduces key essays from this high moment of structuralism in its Lacano-Althusserian iteration and also includes interpretative essays and interviews with surviving members and affiliates of the project.

B. Han, *Foucault's Critical Project: Between the Transcendental and the Historical* (Stanford, CA: Stanford University Press, 2002). An illuminating assessment of Foucault's work that stresses its philosophical dimensions and in particular the dilemmas stemming from its conflicted relationship to neo-Kantianism.

W. Montag, *Althusser and His Contemporaries: Philosophy's Perpetual War* (Durham, NC: Duke University Press, 2013). An engaging assessment of Althusser's project that is especially good at showing how much philosophy of the moment was a response to it.

Chapter 7: French philosophy today: competing ambitions

W. Breckman, *Adventures of the Symbolic: Post-Marxism and Radical Democracy* (New York: Columbia University Press, 2015). A synoptic account of the movements identified in its subtitle that ultimately endorses Lefort's articulation of post-Marxism against competing variants.

J.-P. Deranty and Alison Ross, eds., *Jacques Rancière and the Contemporary Scene: The Philosophy of Radical Equality* (London: Continuum, 2012). Where most of the emerging studies of Rancière focus on one aspect of his work, the main virtue of the essays in this volume is to link multiple aspects of his project with other tendencies in contemporary and historical European philosophy.

T.R. Dika and W. Chris Hackett, *Quiet Powers of the Possible: Interviews in Contemporary French Phenomenology* (New York: Fordham University Press, 2016). A collection of interviews rather than a study, this volume is helpful for providing a non-polemical overview of French phenomenology today in all its tendencies.

P. Hallward, *Badiou: A Subject to Truth* (Minneapolis: University of Minnesota, 2003). Despite an explosion of writing on Badiou, and its being written prior to the appearance of the sequels to *Being and Event*, this first major study of Badiou's work in English remains valuable for the clarity of its presentation and the way in which it situates his project among multiple strands of influence in French intellectual history, from modernist aesthetics to radical politics.

I. James, *The New French Philosophy* (Cambridge: Polity Press, 2012). A remarkably accessible volume despite the difficulty of the material in question, this book provides chapter overviews of contemporary French philosophers oriented around the notion of philosophy as a 'technique of thought'.

J. Mullarkey, *Post-Continental Philosophy: An Outline* (London: Continuum, 2007). Less accessible, this volume is interesting for the way in which it interprets Badiou, Deleuze, and Henry, along with the 'non-philosopher' François Laruelle, in a common frame concerned with the ontological problem of immanence.

Index

For the benefit of digital users, indexed terms that span two pages (e.g., 52–53) may, on occasion, appear on only one of those pages.

French Philosophy

French Philosophy

AFRICAN HISTORY
A Very Short Introduction
John Parker & Richard Rathbone

Essential reading for anyone interested in the African continent and the diversity of human history, this *Very Short Introduction* looks at Africa's past and reflects on the changing ways it has been imagined and represented. Key themes in current thinking about Africa's history are illustrated with a range of fascinating historical examples, drawn from over 5 millennia across this vast continent.

'A very well informed and sharply stated historiography...should be in every historiography student's kitbag. A tour de force...it made me think a great deal.'

Terence Ranger,
The Bulletin of the School of Oriental and African Studies

www.oup.com/vsi

CRITICAL THEORY
A Very Short Introduction
Stephen Eric Bronner

In its essence, Critical Theory is Western Marxist thought with
the emphasis moved from the liberation of the working class to
broader issues of individual agency. Critical Theory emerged
in the 1920s from the work of the Frankfurt School, the circle
of German-Jewish academics who sought to diagnose--and, if
at all possible, cure--the ills of society, particularly fascism
and capitalism. In this book, Stephen Eric Bronner provides
sketches of famous and less famous representatives of the
critical tradition (such as George Lukács and Ernst Bloch,
Theodor Adorno and Walter Benjamin, Herbert Marcuse and
Jurgen Habermas) as well as many of its seminal texts and
empirical investigations.

www.oup.com/vsi

EXISTENTIALISM
A Very Short Introduction
Thomas Flynn

Existentialism was one of the leading philosophical movements of
the twentieth century. Focusing on its seven leading figures,
Sartre, Nietzsche, Heidegger, Kierkegaard, de Beauvoir,
Merleau-Ponty and Camus, this *Very Short Introduction* provides
a clear account of the key themes of the movement which
emphasized individuality, free will, and personal responsibility
in the modern world. Drawing in the movement's varied
relationships with the arts, humanism, and politics, this book
clarifies the philosophy and original meaning of 'existentialism' -
which has tended to be obscured by misappropriation. Placing
it in its historical context, Thomas Flynn also highlights how
existentialism is still relevant to us today.

www.oup.com/vsi

FRENCH LITERATURE
A Very Short Introduction
John D. Lyons

The heritage of literature in the French language is rich, varied, and extensive in time and space; appealing both to its immediate public, readers of French, and also to aglobal audience reached through translations and film adaptations. *French Literature: A Very Short Introduction* introduces this lively literary world by focusing on texts - epics, novels, plays, poems, and screenplays - that concern protagonists whose adventures and conflicts reveal shifts in literary and social practices. From the hero of the medieval *Song of Roland* to the Caribbean heroines of *Tituba, Black Witch of Salem* or the European expatriate in Japan in *Fear and Trembling*, these problematic protagonists allow us to understand what interests writers and readers across the wide world of French.

GERMAN PHILOSOPHY
A Very Short Introduction
Andrew Bowie

German Philosophy: A Very Short Introduction discusses the idea that German philosophy forms one of the most revealing responses to the problems of 'modernity'. The rise of the modern natural sciences and the related decline of religion raises a series of questions, which recur throughout German philosophy, concerning the relationships between knowledge and faith, reason and emotion, and scientific, ethical, and artistic ways of seeing the world. There are also many significant philosophers who are generally neglected in most existing English-language treatments of German philosophy, which tend to concentrate on the canonical figures. This *Very Short Introduction* will include reference to these thinkers and suggests how they can be used to question more familiar German philosophical thought.

www.oup.com/vsi

TOCQUEVILLE
A Very Short Introduction
Harvey Mansfield

No one has ever described American democracy with more accurate insight or more profoundly than Alexis de Tocqueville. After meeting with Americans on extensive travels in the United States, and intense study of documents and authorities, he authored the landmark *Democracy in America*, publishing its two volumes in 1835 and 1840. Ever since, this book has been the best source for every serious attempt to understand America and democracy itself. Yet Tocqueville himself remains a mystery behind the elegance of his style. In this *Very Short Introduction*, Harvey Mansfield addresses his subject as a thinker, clearly and incisively exploring Tocqueville's writings-not only his masterpiece, but also his secret *Recollections*, intended for posterity alone, and his unfinished work on his native France, *The Old Regime and the Revolution*.

www.oup.com/vsi

SOCIAL MEDIA
Very Short Introduction

Join our community
www.oup.com/vsi

- Join us online at the official Very Short Introductions **Facebook** page.
- Access the thoughts and musings of our authors with our online **blog**.
- Sign up for our monthly **e-newsletter** to receive information on all new titles publishing that month.
- Browse the full range of Very Short Introductions online.
- Read **extracts** from the Introductions for free.
- Visit our library of **Reading Guides**. These guides, written by our expert authors will help you to question again, why you think what you think.
- If you are a teacher or lecturer you can order inspection copies quickly and simply via our website.

ONLINE CATALOGUE
A Very Short Introduction

Our online catalogue is designed to make it easy to find your ideal Very Short Introduction. View the entire collection by subject area, watch author videos, read sample chapters, and download reading guides.